No Green Thumb R

Everyone wants their family to eat healthy food and a back yard garden is the way to go. But with today's big houses and tiny yards, often there is no room for a traditionally sized garden. Most families are too busy to take on a project that requires hours of weeding every week nor do they have the time to research planting dates and plant varieties.

"No Green Thumb Required" is a new approach to home gardening that combines ancient methods of intensive gardening with the latest research in soil science, natural fertilizers, and organic gardening techniques.

Best of all, it's easy! By building raised beds and filling them with weedless soil, you eliminate the hassle. All you do is plant seeds and water as needed. This book will take you through the steps of how you and your family can plan, install and manage your own organic garden, and save money on vegetables at the supermarket, too!

Start a new tradition in your family, help your kids learn about nature, and start eating, safe, fresh, healthy vegetables, all year long!

This book is dedicated to my parents,
Carol and Morton Rosenberg,
who have supported me throughout
my entrepreneurial career,
and my two sons, Jeffrey and David,
whose excitement with digging up sweet potatoes,
carrots and beets inspired me to share my love of
vegetable gardening with other families.

No Green Thumb Required!

Organic Family Gardening Made Easy

Don Rosenberg

Rosenberg, Don.
No Green Thumb Required! Organic Family Gardening
Made Easy/ Don Rosenberg
            p. cm.

ISBN 978-1-59712-299-3 $24.95
1. Vegetable Gardening.

First Printing 2009

Printed in the United States of America
printed by Catawba Publishing Company, Charlotte, NC

Cover design, Brinkley Design, Charlotte, NC
Plant descriptions and back cover images courtesy of *Seed Savers
Exchange*, Decorah, Iowa.

for distribution information contact
sales@instantorganicgarden.com 704-364-1784

30091345

CONTENTS

Kids' Projects...

Introduction

Raising a family in today's world is a constant series of challenges. Often both parents work or the children live with a single parent. Many families have to take on second or even third jobs. Kids are faced with so many unhealthy choices for their diets that obesity is becoming an epidemic across the country. And when parents try to serve healthy vegetables, they have concerns about toxins from pesticides and diseases that are spread through modern processing methods.

Many parents would like to plant vegetable gardens in their back yards, but don't have the time to do all the work associated with traditional ones, nor do they have the knowledge and expertise on what to grow or how to manage them successfully. Often they have a big house with a tiny yard and don't have room or they live in an older neighborhood with a large back yard, with lots of trees and only a limited area with adequate sunlight.

The good news is that there is a new approach to home gardening that is both organic and easy.

The good news is that there is a new approach to home gardening that is both organic and easy. It combines ancient techniques of intensive, terrace gardening to conserve space and maximize harvest, with the latest research on soils, organic fertilizers, and safe methods of insect and disease control. By planning properly, families can now have an organic vegetable garden in their back yard that produces 80% of the food in 10% of the space with no weeding, digging or tilling.

This book will take you through the steps of how you and your family can plan, install and manage your own organic garden. Because the garden space is much smaller, the workload is almost non-existent. The work you do in your back yard garden will be planting seeds once a season, and watering, usually twice a week. This becomes the perfect family project. Your children won't dread visiting the garden and helping out. Instead they'll see it as a fun activity where everyone is learning about different vegetables and how they taste. Even the busiest parents will have time to keep up with their back yard garden.

I've found that when children are involved in planning their garden and planting seeds, they take a personal interest from the very start and often want to check back each day.

They're eager to try the vegetables that result, leading to a lifelong interest in healthy eating and how things grow in nature. Finally, these gardens are a way to build wonderful memories with your children.

Gardening lasts a lifetime. When I was about five years old, I recall sitting on the back porch with my grandfather and shelling peas. They tasted so good, only half of them ended up in the bowl! When he moved to Florida he continued growing vegetables at home. When he passed away I inherited many of his tools. I remember him every time I use his shovel. Now I have clients with gardens whose children can be found munching in the back yard instead of eating cookies and candy.   Don.

Kids' Projects

A major focus of this book on families, since home gardening is a project where everyone can participate. In most chapters I'll have "Kid's in the Garden" tips and tricks for children of all ages.

First, we'll do a quick review of the problems today's families face as they try to provide healthy food for their children...

Chapter 1
The Quest for Healthy Food

Toxins in Foods

Prior to the 1940's, farming was done on a small scale using mostly organic materials. As farms began to consolidate and become larger and larger, small-scale solutions were no longer practical. Instead of tending a diverse group of crops by hand, farmers needed ways to deal with pest problems on a wider scale, especially when working with huge expanses of single crops like corn and wheat. World War II research allowed for the development of all sorts of pesticide and herbicide compounds that ended up being used across the country.

Of course we now know that many of these pesticides stayed within the food itself as well as building up in the environment.

Pesticide Residues in Birds

Chinese scientists have discovered organochlorine residue in sea birds' droppings on the King George Island of Antarctica. Wang Ziqing and Lu Bing, two scientists from the Second Institute of Oceanology under the National Bureau of Oceanography (NBO), released their findings on Friday. Their findings are believed to be one proof that pollution is spreading into Antarctica, supposedly the last pollution-free region on the earth.

The two scientists had collected more than 200 samples of droppings of four species of sea birds and seals in the King George Island where the Great Wall station, Chinese headquarters in Antarctica, is located. According [to] an examination by laboratories in China and Germany, the samples were found to have a high level of organochlorines. Organochlorines have been forbidden in many countries since the 1980s but the impact on the environment is still going on due to residue in the ocean and atmosphere.

Pesticide Residue Found in Bird Droppings on Antarctic Island (Xinhua News Agency July 11, 2003)

Other studies are finding these chemicals in our bodies. Children are particularly at risk. Since large farms can't be weeded by hand, this increases demand for herbicides as well.

Pesticide Residues Found in People

Some 2,500 people were tested in the largest survey ever to see if the pesticides and other chemicals polluting our environment are also polluting our bodies. Levels of 116 chemicals found in food, soil, water, air, or dust were measured to see if they were also in people's bodies (for 89 of them, this was the first survey). This huge undertaking shows the staggering amount of chemicals now in our bodies. It also confirms the results of previous smaller studies: children are at greater risk for higher exposure than are adults. Organophosphate pesticides, for instance, were found at about twice the levels in children's bodies, compared to adults (and remember, even at the same levels children would more likely be harmed).

Also of note, DDT continues to be detected in people in the U.S., even though its use was banned in 1973. The adverse effects of DDT are well-documented. It is particularly devastating to children. In this study, DDT was found in today's children – born long after the ban! The CDC states, "Food is the primary pathway of DDT exposure for the general population." Continued exposure "may be from persisting DDT/DDE in the environment or DDT residues in food." Also, food imported from other countries may still be grown with DDT. Food is the primary pathway for many of the chemicals in the CDC report.

Second National Report on Human Exposure to Environmental Chemicals. Work was done at the CDC's Environmental Health Laboratory.

Name that pesticide.

Take your older kids on a field trip to the garden center and bring a pencil and paper. Stop by the gardening chemicals and see who can write down and pronounce any of the chemical names they find on the labels. Have them stop and notice the odor in the air in that section of the store.

Synthetic Fertilizers

World War II research also yielded synthetic fertilizers. The factories used to develop nitrates for bombs could easily be turned to manufacturing nitrate fertilizers. These compounds tend to leach quickly through the soil and contaminate the water table while leaving salt compounds behind. This has the effect of killing the natural life in the soil, causing problems with the processes of the uptake of nutrition, requiring the use of more and more fertilizer in order to keep up.

We now know that synthetic fertilizers can cause plants to grow in an unnatural manner, resulting in weak stems and leaves, which are more susceptible to insect pests and diseases, furthering the need for pesticides.

Fertilizer Chemicals

While they're at the garden center, stop by the fertilizer section. Have your kids take note of the chemicals used in these materials and compare them with the ingredients in composts and organic fertilizers.

Vicious Cycle

All of these chemical inputs follow each other through a vicious cycle of fertilizers, weak plant growth, pesticides, dying soil and the need for ever more fertilizers. These fertilizers also end up running off into our rivers and streams, causing excessive algae growth, depleting oxygen and killing fish and wildlife.

Contaminated Foods

The mechanization of vegetable production has also led to centralized processing. Crops are harvested in huge lots and brought to massive complexes for processing. A small contamination of *E. coli* at an isolated farm is suddenly spread widely throughout the food supply. And this same conglomeration of harvests means that it's almost impossible to trace back to the source of the contamination.

Salmonella Outbreak

The Centers for Disease Control and Prevention (CDC), the U.S. Food and Drug Administration (FDA) and state/local regulatory officials are working together to investigate an ongoing multi-state outbreak of Salmonella serotype *Saintpaul*. The initial epidemiologic investigation was linked to consumption of raw red plum tomatoes, red Roma tomatoes, round red tomatoes, and products containing these raw tomatoes. However, more recent illnesses have broadened the investigation to include other food ingredients as potential sources of the Salmonella (including jalapeño peppers, serrano peppers, and cilantro). Since mid-April, 1251 persons have become infected with Salmonella Saintpaul in 43 U.S. States, the District of Columbia, and Canada, and, 203 people have been hospitalized. The outbreak is ongoing and about 25-40 new cases are reported each day. This is not the first documented outbreak linking Salmonella with tomatoes. Since 1990, 13 large, multi-state foodborne outbreaks and some small local outbreaks have been associated with different varieties of tomatoes. In the past decade, outbreaks involving contaminated tomatoes made up 17 percent of the total produce-related outbreaks. Salmonella has been the pathogen of concern most often associated with outbreaks involving tomatoes. To date, the economic impact to the fresh tomato industry exceeds $100 million.

Purdue University Food Science July 8, 2008

Food Scares (*For Older Children*)

Next time there's a food poisoning story, have your kids clip out some articles and keep them on hand. Add to your collection as new stories appear. Talk about the importance of washing vegetables and handling food properly.

Organic Food is Safer

We've known from earlier studies that pesticides and toxic chemicals aren't just in the environment – but get into our developing children's bodies. Some kids have high levels and others quite low. What's different between these kids? Is there anything simple and practical that parents can do to lower their own children's risks? In this study children were divided into two groups: those who ate mostly conventional foods and those who ate mostly organic foods. All urine for 24 hours was collected from each child. Children who ate conventional diets had mean pesticide concentrations in their urine 9 times higher than the children who ate organic! Their levels indicated that they had exceeded safe exposure levels set by the EPA and were at increased risk to their health. By contrast, those children who ate organic foods were well within the EPA levels deemed to cause negligible risk. Feeding children organic foods is something simple and practical parents can do right now to protect their children and help them build healthy bodies.

Work was done at the Department of Environmental Health, School of Public Health and Community Medicine, University of Washington. Published October 2002.

Childhood Obesity

Another problem brought about by the mechanization of food production was the huge increase in highly processed flours and sugars and the use of inexpensive corn syrup sweeteners. These are now thought to be a main cause of one of the greatest health concerns today, obesity in children. Our kids are more overweight than ever before and with them running off to school in the morning and eating lunch there, the amount of healthy food they consume is declining rapidly.

Overweight children

In 2002, data showed that 15% of children and teens are considered overweight, a tripling since 1980. An additional 15% of kids and teens are considered "at risk" for becoming overweight.

"More than 75% of children ages 6-11 do not eat the minimum of 3 servings of vegetables or 2 servings of fruit daily."
From How to Teach Nutrition to Kids by Connie Liakos Evers, MS, RD.

Obesity and Disease

300,000 deaths each year in the United States are associated with obesity.

Overweight and obesity are associated with heart disease, certain types of cancer, type 2 diabetes, stroke, arthritis, breathing problems, and psychological disorders, such as depression.

From US Surgeon General.

Vegetable Nutrition and Freshness

Many parents are turning to organic food stores and farmers markets to buy vegetables for their families, but organic produce is becoming more and more expensive and driving to the edge of town every Saturday uses up a lot of gas. But the biggest problem with organic produce and farmers markets is freshness. The average vegetable loses 15% of it's nutritional value every day after it is harvested. So if you buy produce from the store and it was picked five days ago, it has half of the nutritional value of something picked today. Even if the farmer at the market harvested his vegetables the day before, it may be three to nine days before you end up using all you bought.

Soil Fertility and Nutrient Content

Recent studies show that when the same land is used repeatedly for farming the same crops, the micro-nutrients in the soil become depleted. Replacing nitrogen, phosphorous and potassium alone does nothing for these trace elements.

Food Nutrient Content Declining

The amount of nutrients in our food is steadily declining, according to recent research. A recent survey found some fruits and vegetables we buy today contain far fewer nutrients than they did 50 years ago. This is especially noticeable in foods such as potatoes, tomatoes, bananas and apples. Specifically, the potato has lost 100 per cent of its vitamin A, 57 per cent of its vitamin C and iron, and 28 per cent of its calcium.

The study looked at 25 fruits and vegetables, and found that 80 per cent showed drops in calcium and iron, 75 per cent in vitamin A, 50 per cent lost vitamin C and riboflavin, 30 per cent lost thiamine and 12 per cent lost niacin. Data from the US Department of Agriculture also documents a similar trend in vegetables, from the start to the end of the 20th century. The average mineral content of vegetables such as cabbage, lettuce, tomatoes, and spinach has declined from 400 mg to less than 50 mg.

The decline in nutritional content is likely due to changes in farming methods that tend to focus heavily on a food's appearance and ability to be transported and stored effectively. Rather than focusing on vitamin content, food producers are more concerned with high yields, visually appealing product and disease resistance. How foods are cooked and processed may also play a role in diminishing nutrient content. So, today, the diet may not necessarily provide all the vitamins and minerals you need at optimal levels. This has the potential to negatively affect your health, since a number of common diseases are thought to be related to nutritional deficiencies.
News Canada

Organically grown vegetables seem to fare better, probably because farmers who care enough to use organic methods pay much closer attention to soil fertility and composition.

Heirloom Plants More Complete

Research study shows only heirloom organic breeds nutritionally complete.

One look at a big, red tomato and one can almost taste its' juicy freshness...unless, that tomato was part of a group of 43 fruit and vegetable crops analyzed by Dr. Donald Davis, research associate at the Biochemical Institute at the University of Texas, Austin. For two decades, Davis and two colleagues Melvin Epp, and Hugh Riordan analyzed nutritional data taken from selectively bred high yield conventionally grown produce. In 2005, their study titled "Changes in USDA Food Composition Data for 43 Garden Crops, 1950 to 1999" showed the results.

According to Davis, "We tracked 50 years in U.S. Department of Agriculture food composition data for 13 nutrients in 43 garden crops, vegetables, strawberries and three melons. Low and high yield varieties were grown and analyzed side by side eliminating key uncertainties that apply to historical data. The data was then analyzed. "

...What the researchers found were declines in average concentrations of six nutrients. The results of 20 years showed declines in:

protein	6%	calcium	16%
phosphorus:	9%	iron	15%
riboflavin	38%	vitamin C	20%

Declining Nutritional Value of Produce Due to High Yield Selective Seed Breeding. Written by Vicki Godal

Organic vs. Store-Bought

Visit the grocery store with the kids. Have them compare conventional vegetables with their organically grown counterparts. Compare appearance, size, and cost. Buy one of each and do a blind taste test. Does one taste better than the other? Once your garden is productive, have them do the same taste test again. Which is better, store-bought, organic or fresh-picked?

Food Prices

Another problem facing today's families is the ever-increasing cost of food, with fruits and vegetables leading the way. In 2008 the price of produce is estimated to have climbed at twice the rate of inflation, and organic produce can be 25% to 50% higher than conventionally raised food. Simply growing a few crops at home can have a significant impact on your family's budget.

High Food Prices Hit Poor Families Hardest

The cost of living – measured by the Consumer Price Index – rose during the past 12 months at the fastest pace since 1991. The July 2008 price increases reflected, in part, while rising food prices and may rise quickly, they tend to come back down more slowly. Since most families' incomes are not keeping pace with rising costs for everything from food to gasoline, many are facing hard choices – especially those at the bottom of the income ladder...

Differential Impacts on Families
Although it is instructive to look at averages, a better understanding of how recent price increases are affecting families comes from a look across the income range. The budget shares consumed by food vary widely by income. In reality, recent price increases have little impact on those with upper or upper-middle incomes. Using 2006 Consumer Expenditure Survey data to illustrate, families with incomes in the upper 20 percent of the income distribution spend roughly 7 percent of after-tax income on food... Their food bill would have increased during the past year from about $10,300 to $11,000...

In contrast, families in the lowest 20 percent of the income ladder spend nearly one-third of their after-tax income on food and about 10 percent on gasoline and motor oil. Their average food expenditures would have grown from about $3,200 to $3,400... Increases in food prices are felt acutely by poor families on food stamps, the federal food assistance program. In the 12 months ending in May 2008, the cost of food for USDA's minimum nutritional diet had risen 7.2 percent, but food stamp allocations have not changed since last fall and will not rise again until October 2008... Given the growing challenge of stretching the food dollar, it is not surprising that local food pantries are experiencing increasing numbers of requests for supplemental food.

Rising Energy and Food Prices: Effects on Families. Cynthia Needles Fletcher, Department of Human Development and Family Studies

Fossil Fuels Used in Food Production

By now you've heard the average vegetable travels 1500 miles to reach your table. The costs to the environment from all this trucking are massive. Whether you're a believer in man as the cause of global warming or not, reducing the amount of travel involved in food production can only be seen as a positive goal. In 1945, 40% of produce was grown in home gardens. A National Gardening Association survey showed 49% of families reported having a home garden in 1975 during the first oil crisis. Now the number is 22%. Even a small increase in home gardening can have a measurable impact on family food costs and fuel consumption.

Food Miles

"Food Miles" refer to the distance that your food has been transported between its source farm and where you buy it. Food miles are one measure of the amount of energy used to transport your food and the consequent pollutants released by that transport. Estimates vary but transport may account for 20% or more of the total energy use associated with the provision of a given food item. As such, Food Miles are a relatively simple statistic that can be used to demonstrate the ecological importance of local foods.

Seventeen percent of this nation's petroleum consumption is dedicated to on-the-farm food production. Add on processing, packaging, refrigeration and transport of edibles and food takes a big bite out of affordable oil supplies and contributes to pollution. Domestic food as basic as lettuce we could grow in front yards most of the year, and green houses in winter, travels up to 3,000 miles from field to table.
http://www.revivevictorygarden.org/FoodMiles.html

Long Distance Produce

Visit the grocery store produce section and make a list of fruits and vegetables. Later go online and find out where they're grown and how many miles away that is from your house. Identify which of these can be grown in your area, or even your back yard!

Chapter 2
Traditional Gardening Woes

Of course, the solution to the issues I've listed is to start a garden in your back yard and grow your own vegetables. But as you will see, traditional methods of home gardening have their own set of problems...

Family Issues

Families don't spend much time together any more. Children come home from school and start to play on their computers. Parents arrive in time to throw some dinner together, the kids rush through their homework and watch TV and soon everyone is off to bed to have everything start again the next day. There are very few projects around the house that are done as a family. If they were to start a traditional garden, the amount of work planting and managing it is so massive it would become a family chore and a dreaded task instead of something that's fun.

> I met a woman at one of my talks who grew up in a house with a large family garden in the 1960's in the South. She said when her parents would call her and her brothers and sisters outside to weed their thousand square foot garden she used to hide under her bed.   Don.

Limited Garden Space

Many of today's families live in a big house with a small yard. They may want a garden, but they don't have the space they need for one of a traditional size, even one that's only 20 x 20 feet. Or they may have a big house and a big yard, but one that is dominated by mature trees, so there's not enough available sunlight.

Weeds, Weeds, Weeds!

Using the existing soil for a garden is also a problem. Native soils contain weed seeds, which can lay dormant for 20 to 50 years! These weeds always grow faster and stronger than domesticated vegetables, so when you add compost and fertilizer you end up with a weed patch instead of a vegetable garden. The amount of work needed to pull weeds from a new garden bed is one of the main reasons why homeowners shy away from starting one.

Table 1: Relative Viability of Selected Weed Seeds

Common Name	Life Cycle	Seeds per Plant	Relative Seed Longevity (years)
Canada thistle	Perennial	680	3
Green Foxtail	Annual	7,160	3 **
Lambs quarters	Annual	72,450	20+ *
Red root pigweed	Annual	117,400	25-30
Smartweed	Annual	3,140	10-20
Velvetleaf	Annual	~2,000	> 40
Wild buckwheat	Annual	11,900	20+ *
Wild mustard	Annual	13,400	3-5
Wild oats	Annual	250	0-8

Source: Manitoba Agriculture *Conn et al., 2006. Weed Science, Vol. 54, No. 3, pp 464-470

Weed Patrol

Go on a walk through your yard and see how many different weeds you can find. Pull them out and take them inside. Google "identify weeds" and look for some sites or try http://weedid.aces.uiuc.edu/

Contaminated Soils

Using existing soil is also a problem if you're concerned about soil contamination. Many housing developments are being built near landfill areas, dump sites, or old farmland. There's no telling what kind of chemicals, oil, gasoline, lead paints, etc., may have gotten into the soil.

Water Restrictions

In 2007, a drought hit the southeast United States, causing major crop losses, and necessitating water restrictions in states and counties across the country. Homeowners were not allowed to water their lawns and gardens, or even wash their cars. When hand watering was finally allowed, it would take almost an hour to water a traditionally sized 400 square foot garden.

There has been a six-year drought in the southwest states as well. Water levels at Lake Mead in Nevada are down 50 feet in just the past three years. As the demand for water increases it is likely water restrictions will become the norm, not the exception.

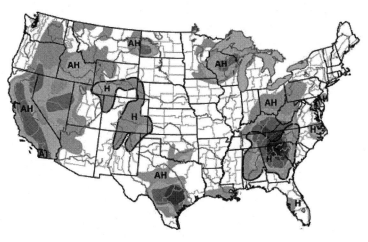

U.S. Drought Monitor, November 2008

Saving Water!

Go on a local TV station's website and look for their weather report section. See if they have a chart that shows average annual rainfall for your area and compare that with actual totals. Talk about water usage in your family and easy ways to conserve water.

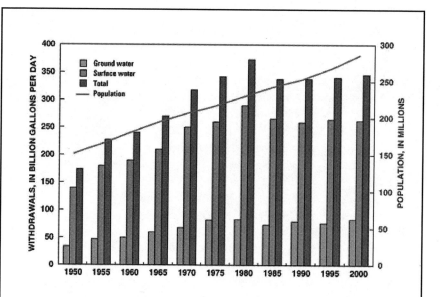

Trends in ground-water use, 1950-2000

Ground water is vitally important in supplying water for our Nation's everyday water needs. Ground water is used to irrigate crops and supply homes, businesses, and industries with water. This bar chart shows America's use of ground and surface water from 1950 to 2000.

The left-side bar in each set of three bars shows the amount of ground-water withdrawals for the United States. Roughly one quarter of the water used in the United States has come from ground water. This proportion has remained fairly constant throughout the last 50 years. The majority of ground water goes towards crop irrigation, with the next largest use being water withdrawn for public-supply purposes (water withdrawn by a government or private agency and delivered to homes and businesses). Ground water is almost exclusively used by people who supply their own home water (self-supplied domestic use).

Data table of trends in water use in the United States 1950-2000.

Chapter 3
Your Back Yard Garden Solution

I'm sure by now the idea of starting a garden in your back yard probably sounds horrible, considering all the work of digging, tilling and weeding. But the purpose of this book is to suggest a new approach to home gardening that is so easy it can be summed up in four words...
"Raised Beds, Weedless Soil."

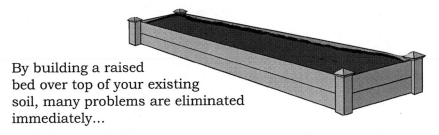

By building a raised bed over top of your existing soil, many problems are eliminated immediately...

1 You never turn over your native soil to expose dormant weed seeds to sunlight, so they never germinate.

2 You eliminate drainage problems since elevated beds drain away unnecessary water.

3 You avoid any contamination from existing soil.

You then fill your raised beds with weedless soil mix and use organic fertilizers...

1 No more need for synthetic fertilizers. You end up with strong, natural, plant growth.

2 Healthy plants resist bugs and diseases, meaning less need for harmful pesticides.

3 Weedless soil eliminates work for you and your family (*weeding is 2/3 of the work in a typical garden*) with no need for herbicides.

4 Since raised beds with super fertile soil are more productive, you can grow more crops in less space using less water. In fact, you can get about 80% of the harvest of a regular 20 x 20 square foot garden in 10% of the space, and that means 10% of the water as well!

Because you are growing your own vegetables in your back yard, you can pick what you want the *hour* before you need it and your vegetables will be at the peak of their nutritional content and flavor!

1 This eliminates concerns about toxins in your foods as well as contamination, since you know what went into your own garden.

2 It maximizes the nutritional value and flavor of your vegetables. Your children may not like everything you grow, but you can be sure it's not because of poor taste!

3 It reduces the amount of fossil fuels needed to produce food for your family.

SAMPLE FARM GARDEN PLAN, 4,000 SF.

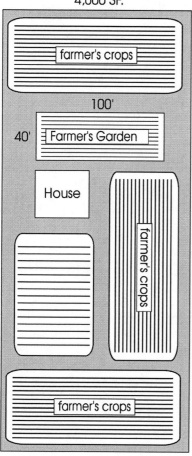

Gardening History

Perhaps you've decided that raised bed gardens might be worth a try, but how can such a small garden be productive enough to be worth the effort?

First, a bit of history is in order...

Gardens have changed over the years. Prior to 1900, most families lived on farms and grew their money crops over the majority of their land. But there was usually a family vegetable plot somewhere on the property, most often near the house. These gardens would be like mini-farms with row crops, just with a wider selection for family use.

A typical garden might be 40 x 100 and would be managed by the wife and kids. These 4,000 square feet would produce much of the food for the family and great effort was spent preserving the extra harvest, through drying or canning.

At the turn of the century, more families were leaving the farms and moving to the cities, but they still wanted their vegetable gardens.

"Victory gardens" were grown from World War I through World War II, but in much smaller spaces, usually a plot of 20 x 20 totaling 400 square feet was enough. In 1945, 40% of produce was grown in these gardens at home, often tended by the wife since the kids were at school.

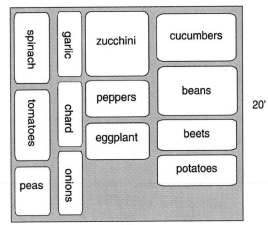

SAMPLE GARDEN PLAN, 400 SF.

Today things have changed. Big houses and tiny yards are the norm. There's no room for even a 400 square foot garden. Families don't have time for digging, tilling, fertilizing and weeding. So most never even give it a try.

A new approach using raised beds and weedless soil can mean a dramatic decrease in workload and get more families back to gardening again.

"Family Farms" Over the Years

Use Google Images to search for "family farm." Discuss the different pictures that show up and print out your favorites. See if the images have changed over time.

Going Organic

Other than the clear benefits of not adding any foreign chemicals into the world than necessary, why is organic gardening better? You may have heard it's harder to grow an organic garden than one using chemicals, but that applies mostly to commercial growers with acres and acres of crops. A home gardener has the time to pay special attention to individual plants if needed.

I'm often asked for a definition of organic gardening. While there are scientific answers, a simple reply is best - *"an organic garden is one where no artificial chemicals are used."* But, in my opinion, organic gardening is more of a way of thinking than a technical definition. Chemical gardens use various materials to react with plants and insects in an unnatural way, while organic gardens use plants' *basic properties* to achieve happy, healthy results.

For example, someone may have a tomato plant that looks a little peeked, so they apply some chemical fertilizer to perk it up. Synthetic fertilizer is like an electric shock to a plant - it grows whether it needs to or not. Usually this growth is spindly and weak, extremely susceptible to insects and diseases. So bugs appear on the tomato plants and our gardener brings out the pesticides, which kill the good bugs as well as the bad bugs, and harm the soil so the plant doesn't get the nutrition it needs. The result is a need for more fertilizers and pesticides. It's a vicious cycle all too common these days.

Organic gardeners have learned that healthy plants resist bugs and diseases naturally, and the key to it all is healthy soil.

Organic gardeners have learned that healthy plants resist bugs and diseases naturally, and the key to it all is healthy soil. Your goal is good, clean soil, with slow-release organic fertilizers, properly balanced pH along with plenty of compost and the right trace elements. This fosters the development of worms and beneficial bacteria and fungi, which allow plants to grow up to be strong and disease-resistant. Healthy plants that grow at the proper pace end up with thick green stems and leaves so they can resist bugs and diseases naturally. And most importantly, healthy soil yields the tastiest vegetables! An organic gardener who visits your garden doesn't only look at your plants. First, he looks at your soil!

Instead of spraying pesticides in advance across the entire garden, we invite beneficial insects and animals to take care of problems naturally as they occur. When there is an issue, it's usually with a single pest on a single crop and we look for an organic solution instead of a one-size-fits-all spray program.

To me, organic gardening is better because it's *easier*. It's simpler to plan in advance for good soil and healthy plants than to have to apply nasty-smelling fertilizers and pesticides constantly. A little bit of thought and preparation will mean a lot less work and better results in the long run.

Chapter 4
Efficient Gardening Approaches

In order to make a small garden pack a big punch, we need to understand some gardening terms...

Intensive Planting

The goal is to generate the highest possible yield over the longest possible period of time. One way to do this is "intensive planting," which is planting more densely than normal. Because the soil we will use is extremely fertile, plants can grow much more closely together than in a normal row garden. If the seed package says "space seeds 12" apart in rows 18" apart, I plan for plants to grow in blocks 6" to 8" apart. The roots grow *down* instead of *out.*

Succession Planting

As one crop comes out, another is put in. This keeps the soil from being bare and open to weeds. It's the best use of small space and fertile soil. If you're heading into another cool season and your crop is starting to decline, you can always plant some more seeds and start your next season's crop. Thin out your remaining plants to one per square foot, smooth out the soil, and plant another batch of seeds.

Companion Planting

Gardeners know and horticultural scientists have proven that certain plants are happier when grown together. Some plants, like those in the onion family, (*garlic, leeks, shallots, etc.*) produce chemicals that discourage other plants from grow-ing. Others help compatible plants to grow. Still other combinations are beneficial because one may deter the pests that bother another plant,

> ### The Three Sisters
> Native Americans have been companion planting for thousands of years. You may have heard of "the three sisters." This is a method of growing corn, beans and squash together that generates a larger harvest than growing them separately. The corn seeds are planted first, and once they're about a foot tall, beans are planted at their base. The beans use the corn as a living trellis and since their roots fix nitrogen into the soil, they benefit the corn as well. Squash seeds are planted in the rows between the corn and beans. This makes efficient use of the space and shades the base of the beans and corn, conserving water.

some may attract beneficial insects, and others can provide shade for their neighbors in the heat of summer.

Inter-planting

Instead of planting in straight rows like we see in larger gardens, we want to put different plant varieties in the same space. This encourages beneficial insects, crowds out and shades out weeds, and gives you a more productive garden.

No Till Gardening

Many people start a summer garden in the middle of April with good intentions, but since weeds are always more vigorous than domestic vegetable plants, so the hotter it gets, the faster they grow. And no one wants to be in the back yard on hands and knees when it's 95° outside!

But how do you prevent a garden from turning into a weed patch? First, you have to understand that weeds are nature's way of quickly covering exposed, bare ground that results from floods, landslides and forest fires. Weed seeds can exist your garden soil for 20 to 50 years, just waiting to see sunlight and sprout. Every time you till your garden, not only do you pulverize the natural layers of your soil, you're also bringing up a fresh batch of weed seeds to torment you all summer.

The solution is to avoid in-ground gardening and build raised beds instead – filling them with weedless soil and organic fertilizers. You go over top of your existing lawn and leave the weeds in the dark and undisturbed so they won't sprout.

Not having to till every year means less work! You don't disrupt the natural layers that develop, and you don't pulverize the soil or ruin its structure.

If you think about it, tilling a garden is a particularly unnatural activity. Look at the plants in a forest. They seem to do very well without any help at all - you don't see Smokey the Bear out with a tiller every spring, do you?

Every season mix organic fertilizer into the top inch or so and mulch every summer with two inches of compost. Instead of tilling it in, let the worms do your tilling for you!

Chapter 5
Getting Started

So you'd like a garden in your back yard. What do you need to check first?

1. Sunlight

You need at least six hours of sunlight each day. It can be morning or afternoon sun, and if you have some partial sun during the day, you need to factor that in, too. *(Half sun for two hours is the same as one hour of full sun.)*

2. Garden Size

Use the *"Goldilocks Rule"* - not too much and not too little. That means you don't want so many vegetables that you scare your neighbors by knocking on their doors trying to give away baskets of tomatoes and zucchini. On the other hand, you should have enough of a harvest each evening to make a meal. I tell clients *"If you're having peas for dinner - you want more than seven."* You'll need to know which vegetables your family members are interested in, how many square feet will be needed to supply an adequate harvest of each crop, and add that up for each season to determine the number and types of beds to build. We'll do all this in upcoming chapters.

How Much Sunlight?

Here's a tip on how to determine your sun... If you have a digital camera, bring your kids out to your back yard in the morning and snap a few photos of the spots you think might work best. Then set your oven timer for one hour and go back out and take the same shots again. Continue this throughout the day. It will give you an accurate record of your sunlight. If you do this in winter or spring, make note of the shadows of any tree trunks, since they'll indicate where the shade will be once the leaves are back. Also note that the sun will be lower in the sky in the winter and fall, so you'll need to take that into consideration.

3. Slopes and Hills

Level ground or a gentle slope is best. If it's a little bit steeper, your garden will have to be terraced into the slope. A proper raised bed garden is either two feet or three feet across, so if your slope doesn't drop by more than 8 or 9 inches in three feet, you should be OK.

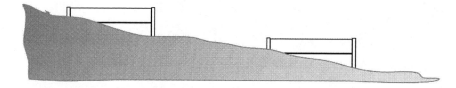

4. Location, Location, Location

You want your garden to face south, with the tallest crops in the back. Since you'll be visiting your garden often, it's best to place it close to your back door and near your water source.

Raised Beds and Trellis Beds

As we have discussed, digging in the soil is a lot of hard work and it brings thousands of dormant weed seeds up to the surface. If your soil is red clay, the area around your in-ground garden bed will hold water like a bathtub. In a period of wet weather your plants can drown or their roots can rot. Raised beds have been used for thousands of years for growing lots of vegetables in small spaces. They offer better drainage and resist weeds. The few weeds you will have are easy to pull. Tending plants takes less work, and harvesting is a breeze. Raised beds eliminate soil compaction. They heat up faster in the spring and stay warmer in the fall, adding as many as three weeks to your growing season. Finally, they're easy to water.

Growing Vertically

Because our garden's footprint is small we need to get the best use out of our limited space. The solution is to grow vertically. This can be something as simple as "the three sisters" of corn, beans and squash I mentioned before, or as complicated as a permanent trellis and netting system that can be used year round. Even growing tomatoes using stakes is a form of vertical growing.

The Benefits of Vertical Gardening

Many crops are affected by disease and fungus problems that are exacerbated by moisture on the leaves. Trellises and stakes increase air circulation, allowing plants to dry out more quickly after a rain. This often eliminates the problems completely.

Plants have greater access to sunlight. When you run your garden east to west and put the trellis and the taller plants in the back, everything gets an even wash of sunlight, whether your sunlight is primarily in the morning or the afternoon.

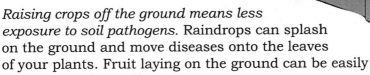

Raising crops off the ground means less exposure to soil pathogens. Raindrops can splash on the ground and move diseases onto the leaves of your plants. Fruit laying on the ground can be easily contaminated as well and is more easily attacked by bugs and critters. Raising the plants also means that beneficial predators have better access to the bugs bothering your garden.

Climbing varieties often taste better! In order to allow for mechanical harvesting, many bush bean and pea varieties were bred to mature at the same time. Taste was not as important as timing. Your harvest period will be longer, too! This also applies to bush tomatoes and cucumbers.

Racing Vines!

Have a competition with different crops and different varieties. Each child can choose a seed and mark it as theirs. Track the results on a chart — first to sprout, first to grow one foot, first to flower, first to harvest. See who has the tallest plant at the end of the season. Do the biggest seeds grow the tallest?

Trellises make crops easier to harvest. No one likes bending down to pick peas or beans. Picking peas, beans or cucumbers at eye level is a pleasure! And having your crops where you can see them means it's a lot easier to tell if something's crawling on them.

Increased leaf surface. Finally, it's not the footprint of your garden that matters, but the amount of leaf surface you can expose to sunlight. A trellis that's seven feet tall and nine feet wide will add 63 square feet of growing surface to a 3' x 9' garden bed.

Crazy Gardens!

As your skills with gardens improve, consider making gardens all over your property using crazy containers. Try old shoes, watering cans, or even rusted out wagons. Remember to poke holes for drainage and use your good potting mix.

If the planters are small add water saver crystals (*available at any garden center*) to help retain moisture so the gardens won't dry out too fast.

Chapter 6
Which crops to grow?
Think "FRESNO"

Because our gardens have limited space we have to make some hard decisions on what's best to grow and what to buy at the local farmers market. I use the word "FRESNO" to help me remember...

F *Tastes better fresh.* All vegetables are much tastier when they're fresh, but some are amazing when compared with frozen, fresh from your local store, or even from a farmers market. That's because many vegetables lose their flavor within hours of being picked. Others are picked before they're ripe and never achieve their full flavor. If you've ever eaten peas fresh out of the pod you're in for a treat. The most popular items in the garden are tomatoes. They're *much* better than "tomatoes" you find in the store.

R *Rare varieties.* Many of the best vegetables can't even be purchased locally. Some good examples are heirloom tomato varieties and yellow sweet potatoes. These are hard for farmers to grow and ship in good condition, so most stores don't even carry them. With your own garden you can grow whatever you want and experiment with unusual and unique varieties.

E *It's expensive in the stores.* As the price of food, especially organic vegetables, continues to climb, it's great to grow vegetables that are the most expensive. Asparagus and blueberries are good examples. Another is baby lettuce mix, which you'll harvest as soon as you start thinning your lettuce seedlings. *(see "Planting Thick and Thin.")*

S *Uses space efficiently.* For our small gardens, we need plants that use their space wisely. Avoid "space hogs" like corn and broccoli, since they take up a lot of room but don't generate a big harvest. A single 3x8 bed planted only with corn might generate 20 ears corn each season. At two for $1 that's a $10 crop! So leave the big crops like pumpkins, watermelons, cantaloupes, melons, and summer squash to local farmers who have plenty of room.

N *Has good nutritional value.* Fresh vegetables have the highest nutritional value at the time of harvest. And vegetables that are grown in complete soil are more nutritious than those from depleted soil. Amend your soil with organic fertilizers that include trace elements. Avoid "empty" vegetables like iceberg lettuce in favor of darker green leafy lettuces.

O *Gives you an ongoing harvest.* Iceberg lettuce makes a large head, you chop it off and you're done. Instead, I advise my clients to grow leaf lettuce. You can plant them a little thicker than normal and then if you thin them as they grow, you have baby lettuce right away. As the plants mature, harvest individual leaves from several plants and have a salad for dinner. You can continue to do this again and again through the rest of the season. Pole beans and climbing peas are also examples of crops with ongoing harvests, especially when compared with bush varieties that were bred to mature at the same time.

As you can see, there are lots of considerations when deciding which plants to grow in your small garden plot. Your goal is to plan the best garden you can, specifically tailored to your family's needs. You want the healthiest, tastiest vegetables and always have something fresh from your garden every night of the week throughout as much of the year as possible. By carefully selecting what you grow you can achieve 80% of the harvest in 10% of the space. A family of four can get excellent results from only fifty square feet.

By carefully selecting what you grow you can achieve 80% of the harvest in 10% of the space. A family of four can get excellent results from only fifty square feet.

In upcoming chapters we'll discuss how to get your kids involved, and determine the best planting times for your area. You'll work out exactly which varieties your family would like to grow so you can lay out your planting plan for the next few seasons. This will tell you how large your garden will need to be and which kinds of beds you'll need.

Chapter 7
Gardening with your kids

Having a vegetable garden in your back yard is a great way to spend quality time with your kids. You'll learn a lot from the experience. Everyone wants their children to eat healthy food, and fresh vegetables taste *much* better than anything you can buy. By getting them involved in the garden they'll be much more willing to try new tastes. The key is to plan in advance so you'll have a good time.

Building a raised bed and filling it with a high-quality potting mix will eliminate hours of digging and weeding. There's nothing that makes a child (*or parent*) lose interest in gardening more quickly than hour-long weeding sessions three days a week!

Use this book to help decide what you want to grow so you'll know the proper planting times and how many plants you'll need for a sufficient harvest. You don't want 30 tomatoes a week, nor do you want just 12 string beans.

Garden Planning

Having your children pick out plants they want to grow gets them involved in their new garden from the very start. You'll need to explain that some vegetables, like watermelon and pumpkins, are just too big for a small garden, but promise to take them to the farmers market, or better yet, to a nearby farm. You may designate a specific spot in the garden for each of your children and have them do ALL the work, from planting seeds, plant care, harvesting, and even cooking. Mark the area with colored string and help them make a label, "Sam's Garden" or "Paul's Peas." Their sense of pride at their accomplishment will amaze you!

Planting with Your Kids

Helping build the beds and filling in the soil is a lot of fun, but the most important part is planting transplants and seeds.

Many vegetables (*tomatoes, peppers, eggplants*) are easiest to start as transplants. Show your children how to remove the seedlings carefully from their trays, loosen any compacted roots, and place them in the garden. Once you're happy with the spacing, you can have them pull aside some soil, drop in the plants and press them lightly into the ground. Don't forget to water when you're done and water again each day until they're established.

Other crops are easily grown from large seeds that are just the right size for even small children to plant. These include peas, green beans, lima beans, and squash. Decide where they will grow and hand each child one seed at a time for them to place on the surface. When they're in the right spot, show them the "push and pinch" method. Push the seeds down about a half inch and pinch the soil above so the seeds are covered.

Small seeds can be frustrating for young children to handle.

Small seeds can be frustrating for young children to handle. First, set aside some potting mix. Smooth the soil and show them where those crops will grow by marking out an area for each one. Have an adult evenly sprinkle the seeds on the soil. Your kids can cover the seeds with about ¼" of the potting mix and gently pat them down to establish good soil contact. You'll need to water these tiny seeds lightly once or twice a day for the first seven to ten days in order to ensure good germination - and kids *love* to water gardens!

There's so much your children can learn, whether they're toddlers or teens. Many of my clients home school their children and they find that having a real vegetable garden in their back yard can be a substantial addition to their curriculum. Here are a few important concepts...

Easiest is Not Always Best

Explain how organic gardening compares with "fertilizer and pesticide" gardening. If a plant isn't doing well it's easy to throw on some fast acting fertilizer. But this results in spindly, weak growth that makes the plant susceptible to diseases and insects. Then you have to apply pesticides that kill more beneficial insects than bad ones and reduce the microbial activity in the soil.

The organic solution is to start with healthy soil that encourages healthy, disease and bug-resistant plants. It takes a bit more knowledge of how things work, but it's worth the effort.

It's OK to Fail - Nothing is Perfect
Another valuable lesson is that not everything in the garden is going to go the way you planned it. Plants die, crops fail. It's all part of the experience. Good gardeners learn from their mistakes and try to fix them next year.

Bean Teepees!

Identify a spot in your yard with good sun that's near your main garden. Remove a foot wide strip of grass making a four-foot diameter ring in your lawn. Loosen the soil, adding compost and slow-release fertilizer to make good garden soil. Fashion a teepee with 8' bamboo stakes a foot apart at the bottom and tie them at the top, placing the base firmly into your soil. Leave an opening about two feet wide in the back. Have your kids plant different types of green bean seeds every four inches. They'll need to pull up any weeds that pop up, but they'll easily tell which are beans and which are weeds. As the plants grow help them get started on the poles. After that, they'll climb on their own and grow all the way to the top. The teepee will be a great place for your kids to hide during the heat of summer and they can harvest the beans from the inside!

The Value of Patience
In a world where every TV episode completes a complicated story line in thirty or sixty minutes, your kids can learn a lot from gardens where it may take two weeks for a seed to sprout and two *months* for a harvest.

Gardening Takes Time!

Once you've planted your seeds, start a chart that shows plant height over time. Mark germination, first "true leaves," first flowers, first fruit appearance, first harvest and last harvest dates.

Math in the Garden

Do some real life math problems - pounds of organic fertilizer per square foot, cubic feet of soil in the raised bed, etc. Create a layout of your planting plan. Chart the growth of specific plants and record harvest results.

Science in the Garden

Experiment with different techniques and chart the results. Put one plant in full sun and another in partial sun and measure the outcome. Experiment with different levels of fertilizer or types of soil.

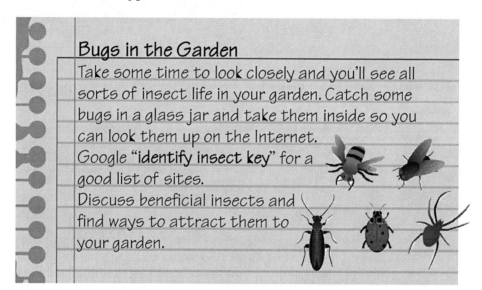

Bugs in the Garden

Take some time to look closely and you'll see all sorts of insect life in your garden. Catch some bugs in a glass jar and take them inside so you can look them up on the Internet. Google "identify insect key" for a good list of sites.

Discuss beneficial insects and find ways to attract them to your garden.

Creating Memories

By far the biggest benefits of gardening with your kids are the memories you'll create. There's nothing more rewarding than the joy and excitement on children's faces as they pull giant sweet potatoes out of the ground, or find a mutant carrot with two legs. These memories will last a lifetime and your kids will end up spending quality time gardening with their own families.

Chapter 8
Organic vs. Heirloom Seeds

My goal is to make organic vegetable gardening so easy that everyone can do it. But I also want to help you save money in your garden and steer you away from products or services that are unnecessary or expensive.

One of the most common questions I hear is "*Are these seeds organic?*" The assumption is that only organic seeds can be used in an organic garden. I'm a huge fan of the

green/organic movement, but I'm disappointed with organic seeds. They are often much more expensive and they give you fewer seeds per package. What makes your garden "organic" are the conditions in which they grow, not whether they were raised on an organic farm. In fact, unless your seeds came from Three Mile Island or Love Canal, they're fine. Just avoid using synthetic fertilizers and pesticides in your garden.

The same applies to buying transplants. Again, they ask, "*Are they organic?*" I recommend using transplants for your summer garden for tomatoes, eggplants and peppers. This allows you to avoid all the work of trying to sprout seeds inside, keeping them alive and hardening them off so they can be planted outside without dropping dead from shock. Some have concerns about transplants, since growers might use synthetic fertilizers in their potting mix. But honestly, once your plant is in the soil, the tiny amount will make no real difference. Buy local transplants and support local growers at nurseries, garden centers and farmers markets, and you'll be able to try several different varieties of each crop.

Organic Seeds, are They Worth the Price?
Buy a package of regular seeds and the same variety as organic seeds. Pour out the seeds from each package and count them. Calculate the cost per seed for both packages and compare.

Heirloom Seeds

One of the problems that came with modern farming is that as newer seed varieties were developed almost all farmers used the same types. They were bred for qualities like shelf life, appearance, durability, and ease of use with mechanical harvesting and processing. Notice I didn't mention TASTE! The result was that many older varieties, which tasted great but didn't grow well on a large-scale farm, were set aside and never grown again.

Several groups have come forward to reclaim these unique historical varieties, usually by acquiring them from home gardeners or established older farms and growing them again as a source of fresh seeds. *Seed Savers Exchange* in Iowa is one of the leaders in the effort. They network with thousands of farmers and home gardeners to gather rare seeds and then sell them to the public to be grown across the country. Their collection is extensive and includes crops like beans carried during the Cherokee Trail of Tears march, beets striped like a bullseye, purple carrots, cucumbers that look like miniature watermelons, and swiss chard with stems in five neon colors.

In the fall of 2008, I began using Seed Savers seeds for all of my customers. These were selected from their extensive catalog for flavor and growing characteristics, but were also chosen based on uniqueness - whether it's appearance, flavor, or a particular seed's rich history. A full list appears later in the book.

On their website, they explain, "*Seed Savers Exchange is a non-profit organization that saves and shares the heirloom seeds of our garden heritage, forming a living legacy that can be passed down through generations. When people grow and save seeds, they join an ancient tradition as stewards, nurturing our diverse, fragile, genetic and cultural heritage. Seed Savers Exchange was founded in 1975 by Diane Ott Whealy and Kent Whealy, to honor this tradition. Their collection started when Diane's terminally-ill grandfather gave them the seeds of two garden plants, Grandpa Ott's Morning Glory and German Pink Tomato, that his parents brought from Bavaria when they immigrated to St. Lucas, Iowa in the 1870s....What a dull world it would be without variety!*" **www.seedsavers.org**

Chapter 9
Determining Planting Dates

It's easy to use the following maps to determine the best planting times for each season for your area. I use the middle of the country as my starting point, so if you're up north you'll plant later and if you're further south you'll plant earlier.

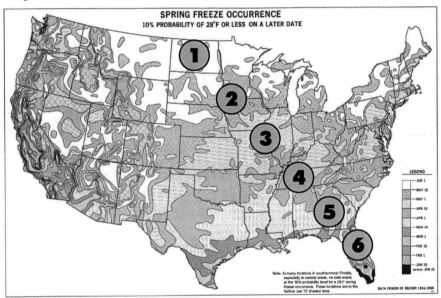

Depending on your zone all you have to do is figure how many days to add or subtract to the planting dates below. So if you live in Indiana, you're probably in Section 3 of the map and you should plant 15 days later than average. Spring seeds should go in around March first and summer seeds and transplants should go out May first. If you can't tell by the map, just Google your city and state and "*last spring frost date.*"

		LAST SPRING FROST ESTIMATED DATES			PLANTING DATES	
					For	Summer
				DAYS	Spring	Seeds and
SECTION	STATES	FROM	TO	+/-	Seeds	Transplants
1	ME, NY, WI, MN, ND, MT	5/15	6/1	-45	4/1	6/1
2	WV, OK, IA, NE	5/1	5/15	-30	3/15	5/15
3	VA, IN, KS, CO	4/15	5/1	-15	3/1	5/1
4	NC, TN, OK	4/1	4/15		2/15	4/15
5	SC, GA, AL, MS, TX	3/15	4/1	15	2/1	4/1
6	FL, LA, TX	3/1	3/15	30	1/15	3/15

The same process applies to fall and winter planting dates... If you live in Wisconsin, you're probably in Section 2 and should plant fall seeds on July first and winter seeds on August first. Again, if you can't tell where you are on the map, just Google city, state and *"first fall frost date."*

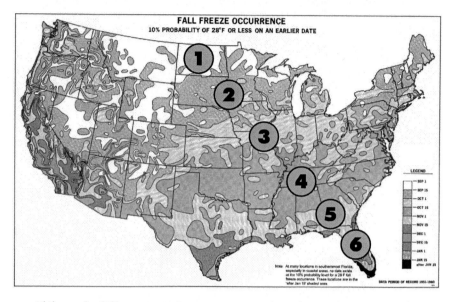

Although different spring crops can be planted at different times according to a complicated plan, my goal is to keep things simple. As long as the soil is warm enough for germination in the spring, and you allow enough time for the crops to mature before summer heat rolls around, planting your entire spring garden at the same time is fine. It's something the entire family can do on a sunny afternoon.

		FIRST FALL FREEZE			PLANTING DATE	
SECTION	STATES	FROM	TO	DAYS +/-	Fall Seeds	Winter Seeds
1	MN, ND, MT	9/1	9/15	45	6/15	7/15
2	ME, VT, NY, WI, SD, WY	9/15	10/1	30	7/1	8/1
3	VA, OK, IN, IA, NE, CO	10/1	10/15	15	7/15	8/15
4	NC, TN, AR, OK, NM	10/15	11/1		8/1	9/1
5	GA, AL, LA, TX	11/1	11/15	-15	8/15	1/0
6	FL, LA, TX	11/15	12/1	-30	9/1	10/1

If you keep good records of your actual planting dates and make note of the results, you'll get a better sense each year as to what's best for your area.

Enter Your Planting Dates Here ...	SPRING	SUMMER	FALL	WINTER

44

Chapter 10
Planning Your Garden

A little bit of planning goes a long way. Use my *"Goldilocks"* rule for deciding how much to plant of a particular crop – *"not too much, not too little."* You don't want so many tomatoes that you scare your neighbors, but you don't want to have peas for dinner and there are only seven.

The idea is to match the supply and the demand for each crop. If you know how many family members like peas, and how many square feet to grow per person, you know the total you'll need. Add all that up for each season and you know how many beds you'll need!

The idea is to match the supply and the demand for each crop.

The following is a list of back yard vegetables I recommend along with notes on specific varieties that are available through *Seed Savers Exchange* as well as other local and online companies.

You'll notice there are some common vegetables that aren't listed; cabbage, corn, cantaloupes, okra, pumpkins, and watermelons. For more information, go back to the chapter about FRESNO, which helps us determine which plants are worth the effort for a home gardener. These simply take up too much room for a limited space home garden. Leave these up to your local farmers and farmers markets! Cabbages aren't recommended because they're not very productive per square foot and they offer only a single harvest. They're inexpensive in the stores and are also a magnet for bugs in the garden.

Your entire family should go through the list together to get a sense of how interested they are in each crop and each variety. Add up the total square feet needed and use it to get an idea of how many beds you'll need. The figures are estimates only. Once you've gone through a season or two in your own garden, you'll have a better sense of how much of each crop to plant.

Mark the varieties you'd like to try. Note the amount of square feet you'll need and add it all up to get a total garden size and a shopping list. Be sure to use a pencil, because you'll make a lot of changes. There are summary pages at the end of the section along with pages for drawing your garden and some sample layouts.

Understanding the charts

I realize that many people suffer from "form-aphobia" and how daunting it can be to fill out an unfamiliar form. Relax! There are seven columns and I've already completed four of them for you. You also know your spring, summer, fall and winter planting dates. Best of all, you don't have to do a thing for any crop you don't want to grow.

Crop vs. variety

First, I talk about each crop in general - what it is, how it's used, basic information. I then list specific varieties, and why I recommend each one.

Number of family members (A)

This is *not* a head count, but how many adults will be using the garden. So mom, dad, a 15-year-old and a two-year-old, are a lot different than a mom with children who are 5, 3 and 1. Our first example might be counted as 3.25 "adults," and the second one might be 2 "adults." So if two adults *love* green beans, and you need two linear feet per person, then you'll need a row four feet long.

Planting date (from the end of Chapter 9)

You just looked this up. For varieties you're interested in, just fill in the planting date for your area for each season.

"Family interest score (B)"

Here's where you rank each crop on a scale of 1 to 10. There are crops you can't get enough of (10), others where you like them most of the time (5), and others you'd like to give a try (2). A big part of the process is figuring out how each family member feels about each crop. So if mom is a big fan of beets and dad won't touch them, that might average out to a score of 5.

Different varieties

In most cases I show recommend varieties on the chart, but I also leave room for you to choose your own. You'll need to divide up your score among your different choices. So if beets are a 6, you might want to put a 2 for Chioggia, a 2 for golden and a 2 for your own choice.

Square feet needed per person (C) (shown)

In the next column I indicate how many square feet are needed to supply one adult.

(D) = SF needed (Adults x BxC)/10

Here's the math! This may seem complicated, but it's just the number of adults, their level of interest in a crop variety, and the number of square feet needed per person, all divided by 10. So if two adults give "dragon carrots" an average score of 5 and it takes 2 feet of carrots per person, then you have 5x2, which is 10. Divide that by 10 and you see that 1 square foot of space needed. Try it and see how much sense it makes. *I promise it's easier than it looks!*

Seeds to plant per square foot (shown)

I include this number to help you with planting.

Thin to # per square foot (shown)

Some seeds don't germinate well. You might need to plant 12 spinach seeds when you only need 6 to grow.

Seeds or plants needed (DxE)

This is simple. If you know to plant 8 seeds per foot and you are planting 3 square feet, you'll need 24 seeds.

Days until harvest (shown)

Another useful bit of info provided to help with planning.

This is not an exact science. Think of your garden as an American Idol for plants. You try different crops and varieties for a season and if you don't like one, you vote it off the show. Next season you can audition something else. If you like a crop, but don't have enough, just plant more next time. Eventually you'll end up with a garden full of your favorite plants, but keep an eye out for new varieties!

Veggie Auditions

Set up an American Idol competition for different varieties of the same crops, like Dragon Carrots and Scarlet Nance Carrots, or Purple Podded Beans and Cherokee Trail of Tears Beans.

Make a list of the qualities you're looking for, like germination rate, maturity time, length of harvest and flavor. Keep close records over the growing season. At the end of the season have a vote as to which varieties you should stick with and where you'll need new contestants!

Chapter 11
Garden Planners

Here it is, the list of crops and varieties I recommend. *To see color images of each variety, go to my website at www.instantorganicgarden.com and click "Online Veggie Quiz."*

Once your family has gone through the list and made notes on each crop of interest, take a separate sheet of paper and make a summary for each season. I have some garden planner summary pages at the end of the chapter.

You don't need to do every season at first, just the next cool season and the summer garden. You're only going to have eight to twelve crops per season, so this shouldn't be a lot of work to summarize. Also make note of which are climbing plants and which will need staking (*tomatoes, peppers, eggplants.*) If you have 8 feet of climbing plants, that means one of your beds should have a trellis.

Garden layouts

I've also created some worksheets for 3x9 trellis and 3x9 raised beds. I show the relative sizes of the larger plants like tomatoes and peppers so you'll know how much room to allocate for each plant. Take the planner for each season and the layout and try to see how everything will fit. It may take a few tries, so use pencil. Better still, make copies of the blank layouts so you can experiment as much as you want. *Sample garden layouts are also included.*

We discussed the "Three Sisters" earlier. If you have 18 feet of climbing plants in your summer garden plan and only 9 feet for the cool seasons, make a temporary "live" trellis in one bed to grow your pole beans. Use a sturdy variety of corn and give the plants a two week head start before you plant the beans. This way you'll only need one permanent trellis bed.

Don.

Garden Planning Worksheets - Arugula to Turnips

(Some variety descriptions courtesy of Seed Savers Exchange.)

Arugula is a green with a bright taste most often used in salads.

Arugula Apollo

Highly improved Dutch strain of domesticated rocket. Very large, rounded leaves are high in vitamin C. Excellent taste and rarely bitter. Will produce 3-5 cuttings per year if kept well picked.

place seeds at a rate of 8 per square foot and thin to 4

Arugula	Suggested Varieties and Planting Info	Family Interest Score (B)	square feet needed per person (C)	(D) = SF Needed (Adults x BxC) /10	Seeds, plants, bulbs etc. to plant per square foot (E)	Thin to # of plants per square foot	Seeds, plants, etc. Needed (DxE)	Approx. days to harvest
SPRING PLANTING DATE	/							
Arugula	Apollo		2		8	4		45
Arugula - Your Variety			2		8	4		45
FALL PLANTING DATE	/							
Arugula	Apollo		2		8	4		45
Arugula - Your Variety			2		8	4		45
WINTER PLANTING DATE	/							
Arugula	Apollo		2		8	4		45
Arugula - Your Variety			2		8	4		45

Asparagus are a perennial vegetable, which means they take up space in your garden all year long, but a bed will produce crops for up to thirty years.

Asparagus - Jersey Giant Crowns

Use two year old male Jersey Giant plants and plant them close together in the spring or fall. This will produce a lot in a small amount of space, but the spears won't become thick and tough over the years.

Asparagus (crowns) Suggested Varieties and Planting Info	Family In-terest Score (B)	square feet needed per person (C)	(D) = SF Needed (Adults x BxC)/10	Seeds, plants, bulbs etc. to plant per square foot (E)	Thin to # of plants per square foot	Seeds, plants, etc. Needed	Approx. days to harvest
PERENNIAL. Plant crowns 5" apart 6" deep, spread out roots.							
SPRING PLANTING DATE /							
Asparagus (crowns) Jersey Giant Crowns		2		8	4		annual
Asparagus - Your Variety		2		8	4		annual
FALL PLANTING DATE /							
Asparagus (crowns) Jersey Giant Crowns		2		8	4		annual
Asparagus - Your Variety		2		8	4		annual

Beans, Green Beans

We prefer pole beans because they offer a better flavor, a longer harvest and they're easier to pick. Plant them in a straight row beneath your trellis..

Cherokee Trail of Tears Bean

Given to Seed Savers Exchange in 1977 by the late Dr. John Wyche, SSE member from Hugo, OK. Dr. Wyche's Cherokee ancestors carried this bean over the Trail of Tears, the infamous winter death march from October 1838 in the Smoky Mountains to March 26, 1839 in Oklahoma, leaving a trail of 4,000 graves. Shiny jet-black seeds. Green 6" pods with purple overlay, good for snaps and dry beans.

Beans, Green Beans, Pole - Purple Podded Pole

Heirloom variety discovered by Henry Fields in an Ozark garden in the 1930s, probably northern European origin. Plants climb vigorously to 6' and are extremely productive. High quality, meaty, stringless 1/2" thick by 5-7" long reddish-purple pods that blanch to light green. This is a fun variety. Pods are a rich purple, but turn a bright green when boiled. Great flavor.

Scarlet Runner Beans have beautiful red flowers and attract hummingbirds like crazy! Great bean flavor.

Beans, Green Beans, Pole	Suggested Varieties and Planting Info	Family Interest Score (B)	square feet needed per person (C)	(D) = SF Needed (Adults x BxC)/10	Seeds, plants, bulbs etc. to plant per square foot (E)	Thin to # of plants per square foot	Seeds, plants, etc. Needed	Approx. days to harvest
plant one seed every 3 inches in rows under trellis	/							
SUMMER PLANTING DATE								
Beans, Green Beans, Pole	Cherokee Trail of Tears		2		4	4		70
Beans, Green Beans, Pole	Purple Podded		2		4	4		70
Beans, Green Beans, Pole	Scarlet Runner Beans		2		4	4		70
Beans, Green Beans, Pole - Your Variety			2		4	4		70
Beans, Green Beans, Pole - Your Variety			2		8	4		70

Beets

Beet "seeds" are actually four seeds together, so plan for some thinning.

Beets - Bull's Blood Beet. Selected by seedsman Kees Sahin in the Netherlands from the French variety Crapaudine for the darkest- colored leaves. Remarkably sweet, 35 days for baby leaf tops.

Beets - Burpee's Golden Beet. Introduced to gardeners before 1828. Dual purpose beet for roots and greens. Roots are globe-shaped and orange, turning golden yellow when cooked. Tender and mild even when large. Great for salads since the sliced roots do not bleed. Sweet, flavorful leaves.

Beets - Chioggia Beet. First introduced to American gardeners in the lat 1840s from Italy. Uniquely beautiful flesh has alternating red and white concentric rings that resemble a bull's-eye. Very tender, nice for eating and pickling. Retains markings if baked whole and sliced just before serving. A spectacular variety.

Beets	Family Interest Score (B)	square feet needed per person (C)	(D) = SF Needed (Adults x BxC)/10	Seeds, plants, bulbs etc. to plant per square foot (E)	Thin to # of plants per square foot	Seeds, plants, etc. Needed (DxE)	Approx. days to harvest
Suggested Varieties and Planting Info							
place seeds at a rate of 5 per square foot - thin as needed	/						
SPRING PLANTING DATE							
Beets, Blood Red	Bull's Blood	1.5		5	5		60
Beets, Golden	Burpee's Golden	1.5		5	5		60
Beets, Red - Striped	Chioggia	1.5		5	5		60
Beets, Red - Your Variety		1.5		5	5		60
Beets, Red - Your Variety		1.5		5	5		60

Beets	Family Interest Score (B)	square feet needed per person (C)	(D) = SF Needed (Adults x BxC)/10	Seeds, plants, bulbs etc. to plant per square foot (E)	Thin to # of plants per square foot	Seeds, plants, etc. Needed (DxE)	Approx. days to harvest
Suggested Varieties and Planting Info							
place seeds at a rate of 5 per square foot - thin as needed							
FALL PLANTING DATE /							
Beets, Blood Red		1.5		5	5		60
Beets, Golden		1.5		5	5		60
Beets, Red - Striped		1.5		5	5		60
Beets, Red - Your Variety		1.5		5	5		60
Beets, Red - Your Variety		1.5		5	5		60
WINTER PLANTING DATE /							
Beets, Blood Red		1.5		5	5		60
Beets, Golden		1.5		5	5		60
Beets, Red - Striped		1.5		5	5		60
Beets, Red - Your Variety		1.5		5	5		60
Beets, Red - Your Variety		1.5		5	5		60

Blackberries

Blackberries are a member of the bramble family and grow well all over the country. Instead of needing fertile garden soil, they grow in native soil and can be placed anywhere in your landscape with good sun. Plan to support them with a simple wire trellis. Available locally as transplants or by mail order as bare root plants. Plant two feet apart. Two plants per person.

Blueberries

Blueberries are one of the best crops to grow in your back yard. They taste fantastic, they are very good for you, and they seem to get more and more expensive in the store every year. They grow as a perennial in your landscape in soil that is amended with peat moss or other material to raise the acidity. You'll want to grow several varieties which ensures better pollination, and, if you choose the right plants, allows for a longer harvest period. Usually available locally as transplants only or by mail order. *See Appendix for blueberry growing tips.* One plant per person.

Broccoli

Very popular in home gardens, but most varieties take up a lot of room and don't yield very much.

Broccoli - DeCicco Broccoli

Introduced to U.S. gardeners in 1890. Compact 2-3' plant produces 4" central head. After the central head is cut, many side shoots follow. Very early, great for freezing.

Broccoli	Suggested Varieties and Planting Info	Family Interest Score (B)	square feet needed per person (C)	(D) = SF Needed (Adults x BxC)/10	Seeds, plants, bulbs etc. to plant per square foot (E)	Thin to # of plants per square foot	Seeds, plants, etc. Needed (DxE)	Approx. days to harvest
Choose only compact varieties	/							
SPRING PLANTING DATE								
Broccoli	DeCicco		2		4	1		85
Broccoli -Your Variety			2		4	1		85

Broccoli	Suggested Varieties and Planting Info	Family Interest Score (B)	square feet needed per person (C)	(D) = SF Needed (Adults x BxC)/10	Seeds, plants, bulbs etc. to plant per square foot (E)	Thin to # of plants per square foot	Seeds, plants, etc. Needed (DxE)	Approx. days to harvest
Choose only compact varieties	/							
FALL PLANTING DATE	/							
Broccoli	DeCicco		2		4	1		85
Broccoli -Your Variety			2		4	1		85
WINTER PLANTING DATE	/							
Broccoli	DeCicco		2		4	1		85
Broccoli -Your Variety			2		4	1		85

Broccoli Raab

Greens described as tasting like a cross between broccoli and asparagus. Although it has broccoli's name, the two are not related. Instead, it is in the turnip family which is probably why the leaves look like turnip greens. Lots of broccoli-like buds appear here and there but a head never forms. It is grown as much for its long-standing, tasty mustard-like tops as for their multiple small florets with clusters of broccoli-like buds. Good quality broccoli raab will have bright-green leaves that are crisp, upright, and not wilted. Avoid ones with leaves that are wilted, yellowing, or have dark green patches of slime.

Used extensively in Italian and Chinese cooking, the stems are generally uniform in size (hence cook evenly) and need not be peeled. This vegetable is a source of vitamins A, C, and K, as well as potassium. Broccoli raab is also known by such names as raab, rapa, rapini, broccoli turnip, spring broccoli, taitcat, Italian turnip, and Italian mustard.

Bussels Sprouts

You either love them or hate them. **They are a winter crop that is started with the fall planting.**

Long Island Improved Brussel Sprout

Harvest the lower sprouts (small heads) when they are about 1 to 1 1/2 inches in diameter by twisting them off. Lower leaves along the stem may be removed to hasten maturity.

This variety is the chief commercial sprout until the development of more uniform hybrids. It generates a heavy set of firm sprouts over an extended period. Compact 20-24" plants yield 50-100 dark-green 1¼ - 1½" sprouts. Introduced in the 1890s.

plant 4 seeds per foot and thin to 2.

Bussels Sprouts	Suggested Varieties and Planting Info	Family Interest Score (B)	square feet needed per person (C)	(D) = SF Needed (Adults x BxC)/10	Seeds, plants, bulbs etc. to plant per square foot (E)	Thin to # of plants per square foot	Seeds, plants, etc. Needed (DxE)	Approx. days to harvest
FALL PLANTING DATE	/							
Bussels Sprouts	Long Island Improved		2		4	2		95
Bussels Sprouts - Your Variety			2		4	2		95

Carrots

Harvest when the roots are 3/4 to 1 inch in diameter. The largest roots generally have the darkest tops. A favorite for kids in the garden. They love pulling them up, not knowing what they'll uncover! They take six months to mature so you want to plan for a constant "carrot patch." You won't plant every season, just plant more seeds as you harvest mature plants. *See Appendix for growing tips.*

Carrots - Dragon Carrot

The finest, most refined purple carrot available, grown and maintained by Dr. John Navazio. One of the best selling carrots at specialty and farmers' markets. The beautiful reddish-purple exterior provides an amazing contrast with the yellowish-orange interior when peeled or sliced. Sweet, almost spicy flavor.

Carrots - Scarlet Nantes Carrot

Cylindrical roots are 7" long by 1½" wide. Bright reddish-orange flesh, fine grained, nearly coreless, great flavor, sweet and brittle. Good as baby carrots. Good for storage, freezing and for juice. Widely adapted, highly selected, uniform strain.

place seeds where indicated at a rate of 20 per square foot. Harvest thinnings.

Carrots	Suggested Varieties and Planting Info	Family Interest Score (B)	square feet needed per person (C)	(D) = SF Needed (Adults x BxC)/10	Seeds, plants, bulbs etc. to plant per square foot (E)	Thin to # of plants per square foot	Seeds, plants, etc. Needed (DxE)	Approx. days to harvest
SPRING PLANTING DATE	/							
Carrots - Purple	Dragon Carrot		2		20	10		90
Carrots - Orange	Scarlet Nantes		2		20	10		90
Carrots - Your Variety			2		20	10		90
Carrots - Your Variety			2		20	10		90

Carrots

	Suggested Varieties and Planting Info	Family Interest Score (B)	square feet needed per person (C)	(D) = SF Needed (Adults x BxC)/10	Seeds, plants, bulbs etc. to plant per square foot (E)	Thin to # of plants per square foot	Seeds, plants, etc. Needed (DxE)	Approx. days to harvest
	/							
FALL PLANTING DATE	/							
Carrots - Purple	Dragon Carrot		2		20	10		90
Carrots - Orange	Scarlet Nantes		2		20	10		90
Carrots - Your Variety			2		20	10		90
Carrots - Your Variety			2		20	10		90
WINTER PLANTING DATE	/							
Carrots - Purple	Dragon Carrot		2		20	10		90
Carrots - Orange	Scarlet Nantes		2		20	10		90
Carrots - Your Variety			2		20	10		90
Carrots - Your Variety			2		20	10		90

place seeds where indicated at a rate of 20 per square foot. Harvest thinnings.

Collard greens

Collard greens date back to prehistoric times, and are one of the oldest members of the cabbage family, but are also close relatives to kale. Although they are available year-round they are at their best from January through April. They last nicely through the winter in most climates.

Collard Greens

place seeds at a rate of 6 per square foot and thin to 2

Suggested Varieties and Planting Info	Family Interest Score (B)	square feet needed per person (C)	(D) = SF Needed (Adults x BxC)/10	Seeds, plants, bulbs etc. to plant per square foot (E)	Thin to # of plants per square foot	Seeds, plants, etc. Needed (DxE)	Approx. days to harvest
SPRING PLANTING DATE /							
Collard greens		2		6	2		40
FALL PLANTING DATE /							
Collard greens		2		6	2		40
WINTER PLANTING DATE /							
Collard Greens		2		6	2		40

Cucumbers

Cucumbers come in bush and pole varieties. The bush plants offer a single harvest over a short time, while the climbing ones will produce all summer long. Harvest when the fruits are deep green, before yellow color appears. The length should be 2 to 3 inches for sweet pickles, 5 to 6 for dills, and 6 to 8 for slicing. Pick 4 to 5 times per week to encourage continuous production. Mature cucumbers left on the vine will stop production of the entire plant.

Cucumber problems... Bitter cucumbers? -- Older plants, low fertility, drought conditions, and high temperatures contribute to bitterness in cucumbers. Maintaining adequate moisture, mulching the soil, and fertilizing properly will delay or possibly prevent bitterness. Most bitterness can be removed by peeling off a thicker portion of the skin during preparation.

Poor fruit set of vine crops? -- Poor pollination is usually the problem. Squash, cucumbers, and other vine crops produce both male and female flowers. It is normal for vine crops to produce 10 or more male blossoms before female blossoms are formed. The male flowers drop without any food production. Bees are needed to transfer the pollen from male to female blossoms.

Double Yield Cucumber - Pickling

Developed by a home gardener and introduced in 1924 by Joseph Harris & Co. of Coldwater, New York. In the words of the introducer, "The remarkable thing about this new cucumber is its wonderful productiveness. For every pickle that is cut off, two or three more are produced." Very productive pickling type. Slender fruits are 5-6" long by 2" in diameter, symmetrical, smooth and uniform.

Japanese Climbing Cucumber - Slicing & Pickling

Introduced to American gardeners in 1892 by Thorburn from seed they obtained from Japan. Vigorous growth, strong grasping tendrils, the best variety we offer for trellises, wire netting, brush or fences. Fruits are 7-9" long by 3" in diameter, light green and of fine quality for both slicing or pickling. Plants continue to bear all season, if consistently picked clean.

Mexican Sour Gherkin Cucumber - for salads

Newly rediscovered heirloom. Produces abundant crops of 1-2" fruits that have the appearance of miniature watermelons, and fall off the vines when ripe. Sweet cucumber flavor, contrasted by a surprising sourness, as if they are already pickled! Great for growing on a trellis.

True Lemon Cucumber - Pickling & Slicing

No, this does not have a lemon flavor! Heirloom that was introduced in 1894 by Samuel Wilson of Mechanicsville, Pennsylvania. Similar in appearance and size to a lemon, averages 3" by 2". Was once a well-established variety in Australian markets. Used primarily for pickling, slicing and in salads. Very easy to digest. Rust and drought resistant, extremely productive.

Cucumbers	Suggested Varieties and Planting Info	Family Interest Score (B)	square feet needed per person (C)	(D) = SF Needed (Adults x BxC)/10	Seeds, plants, bulbs etc. to plant per square foot (E)	Thin to # of plants per square foot	Seeds, plants, etc. Needed (DxE)	Approx. days to harvest
plant one seed every 4 inches along trellis								
SUMMER PLANTING DATE	/							
Cucumbers, pickling	Double Yield Cucumber		1		3	3		45
Cucumbers, slicing	Mexican Sour Gherkin - for salads		1		3	3		45
Cucumbers, slicing & pickling	Japanese Climbing Cucumber		1		3	3		45
Cucumbers, slicing & pickling	True Lemon Cucumber - Pickling & Slicing		1		3	3		45
Cucumbers - Your Variety			1		3	3		45
Cucumbers - Your Variety			1		3	3		45

Eggplants

Harvest when the fruits are 4 to 5 inches in diameter and their color is a glossy purplish black. The fruit is getting too old when the color starts to dull or become bronzed. Because the stem is woody, cut -- do not pull -- the fruit from the plant. A short stem should remain on each fruit.

Florida High Bush Eggplant

Vigorous upright well-branched plants. Large purple fruits with pure-white flesh are held high off the ground. Disease and drought resistant, hardy and everbearing. Dependable variety for market growers.

Listada de Gandia Eggplant

Beautiful striped Italian eggplant. After selecting for over 5 years, this is the best strain out of 10 for color and earliness. Reliable, heavy yields of excellent quality 6-8" thin skinned fruits.

Ping Tung Long Eggplant

Extremely beautiful eggplant that originated in Pingtung, Taiwan. Dark lavender fruits have an incredible shine that radiates off the skin. Slender fruits up to 12" long and just slightly more than 1" in diameter. Hardy, vigorous plants are disease resistant.

Eggplant (plants)	Suggested Varieties and Planting Info	Family Interest Score (B)	square feet needed per person (C)	(D) = SF Needed (Adults x BxC)/10	Seeds, plants, bulbs etc. to plant per square foot (E)	Thin to # of plants per square foot	Seeds, plants, etc. Needed (DxE)	Approx. days to harvest
place transplants 20" apart								
SUMMER PLANTING DATE	/							
Eggplant - Purple Speckled	Listada de Gandia Eggplant		0.7		0.7	0.7		80
Eggplant - Purple Asian	Ping Tung Long Eggplant		0.7		0.7	0.7		80
Eggplant - Purple			0.7		0.7	0.7		80
Eggplant - Your Variety			0.7		0.7	0.7		80

Garlic

Garlic is best planted around mid-October for harvest in the spring. This allows them to overwinter and produce good sized bulbs. You can plant them almost any time to grow garlic greens similar to scallions. Sometimes it's just easier to head to the store and find some nice garlic bulbs and plant those!

Chet's Italian Red Garlic

Highly productive and adaptable strain. Heirloom variety from Chet Stevenson of Tonasket, Washington, found growing wild in an abandoned garden along the roadside. A good garlic for eating raw, because the flavor is not too strong. Softneck, 10-20 cloves per bulb.

Garlic (cloves)	Suggested Varieties and Planting Info	Family Interest Score (B)	square feet needed per person (C)	(D) = SF Needed (Adults x BxC)/10	Seeds, plants, bulbs etc. to plant per square foot (E)	Thin to # of plants per square foot	Seeds, plants, etc. Needed (DxE)	Approx. days to harvest
place cloves 3 inches apart at a rate of 9 per square foot								
WINTER PLANTING DATE	10 / 21							
Garlic (cloves)	Chet's Italian Red Garlic		1		9	9		120
Garlic – Your Variety			1		9	9		120

Kale

Twist off the outer, older leaves when they reach a length of 8 to 10 inches and are medium green in color. New leaves will grow, providing a continuous harvest. Harvest only healthy and well-formed plants, roots, or leaves. Heavy, dark green leaves are too mature and are likely to be tough and bitter. Remove all discolored or damaged leaves. Wash thoroughly in clean water to remove sand and dirt. Does well over winter.

Lacinato Kale

Italian heirloom also known as **Black Tuscan Palm Tree Kale** which dates back to the eighteenth century. Rather primitive, open kale with blue-green strap leaves that are 3" wide by 10-18" long. Heavily savoyed texture, excellent delicious flavor that is enhanced by frost. Leaves are best eaten when small and tender, before fiber develops. Highly nutritious, very ornamental as well as edible. Extremely hardy.

Red Russian Kale

Rare strain, vigorous 18-36" plants have frilly purple-veined blue-green leaves tinged with reddish-purple. Deeply cut margins resemble oak leaves. Very tender, mild sweet flavor. Best used for salads when small. Excellent as boiled greens. Overwinters easily, hardy to -10° F. Quite a sight to see leaves covered with frost. Known since 1885 and reintroduced in 1977 by Canadian herbalist Betty Jacobs.

Kale	Family Interest Score (B)	square feet needed per person (C)	(D) = SF Needed (Adults x BxC)/10	Seeds, plants, bulbs etc. to plant per square foot (E)	Thin to # of plants per square foot	Seeds, plants, etc. Needed (DxE)	Approx. days to harvest
Suggested Varieties and Planting Info							
Twist off the outer, older leaves when they reach a length of 8 to 10 inches and are medium green in color. Heavy, dark green leaves are overmature and are likely to be tough and bitter. New leaves will grow, providing a continuous harvest.							
SPRING PLANTING DATE /							
Lacinato Kale		2		6	3		45
Kale - Purple Stems Red Russian Kale		2		6	3		45
Kale - Your Variety		2		6	3		45
FALL PLANTING DATE /							
Lacinato Kale		2		6	3		45
Kale - Purple Stems Red Russian Kale		2		6	3		45
Kale - Your Variety		2		6	3		45

Kale

Kale	Suggested Varieties and Planting Info	Family Interest Score (B)	square feet needed per person (C)	(D) = SF Needed (Adults x BxC)/10	Seeds, plants, bulbs etc. to plant per square foot (E)	Thin to # of plants per square foot	Seeds, plants, etc. Needed (DxE)	Approx. days to harvest
WINTER PLANTING DATE	/							
Kale - Standard	Lacinato Kale		2		6	3		45
Kale - Purple Stems	Red Russian Kale		2		6	3		45
Kale - Your Variety			2		6	3		45

Kohlrabi

Kohlrabi is a part of the cabbage family. First grown in Europe around 1500, it was imported into America 300 years later. It has a turnip like appearance, with leaves standing out in spokes from the edible portion, which is a rounded, enlarged stem section growing just above the soil line. Kohlrabi is sometimes misclassified as a root vegetable.

Kohlrabi	Suggested Varieties and Planting Info	Family Interest Score (B)	square feet needed per person (C)	(D) = SF Needed (Adults x BxC)/10	Seeds, plants, bulbs etc. to plant per square foot (E)	Thin to # of plants per square foot	Seeds, plants, etc. Needed (DxE)	Approx. days to harvest
Harvest when the thickened stems or bulb (the edible part) is 2 to 3 inches in diameter by cutting off the plant just below the bulb. Stems become woody if left too long before harvest.								
SPRING PLANTING DATE	/							
Kohlrabi - Your Variety	Kohlrabi		1		4	2		55
FALL PLANTING DATE	/							
Kohlrabi - Your Variety	Kohlrabi		1		4	2		55

Leeks

A member of the onion family. Delicious in soups and for a mild onion flavor.

Blue Solaize Leek

French heirloom, truly blue-colored leaves that turn violet after a cold spell. Very large sweet medium-long shaft, extreme cold resistance and hardiness. Good for short-season areas and winter harvest, holds well over the winter in the ground. Beautifully magnificent variety when grown in any garden.

plant seeds at a rate of 4 per square foot. Thin to 2 plant per foot

Leeks	Suggested Varieties and Planting Info	Family Interest Score (B)	square feet needed per person (C)	(D) = SF Needed (Adults x BxC)/10	Seeds, plants, bulbs etc. to plant per square foot (E)	Thin to # of plants per square foot	Seeds, plants, etc. Needed (DxE)	Approx. days to harvest
SPRING PLANTING DATE	/							
Leeks	Blue Solaize Leek		1		4	2		100
Leeks - Your Variety			1		4	2		100
FALL PLANTING DATE	/							
Leeks	Blue Solaize Leek		1		4	2		100
Leeks - Your Variety			1		4	2		100

Lettuce

Lettuce is very popular in the home garden and offers a fantastic variety of colors textures and styles. Avoid head lettuce since it lacks nutritional value and can only be harvested once. Leaf lettuces can be picked early as thinnings and when mature, a leaf at a time, ensuring a long harvest. A healthy choice, especially those with darker color leaves, and expensive fresh and at organic markets. Harvest the older, outer leaves from leaf lettuce as soon as they are 4 to 6 inches long. *See "Planting Thick and Thin" for more tips.*

Lettuce– Bibb Type - Bunte Forellenschuss Lettuce

Harvest heading types when the heads are moderately firm and before seed stalks form. "Bunte" in German means "colorful." Sweet apple-green leaves splashed with maroon, forms and 8-10" loose head. Given to SSE in 1973. Butterhead.

Lettuce – Bibb Type – Pablo

Loose heads form beautiful upright rosettes that look almost like flowers. Wavy-edged flat leaves are extremely wide, sometimes encircling half the head. Good texture, excellent mild flavor. Crisphead.

Lettuce, Bibb	Suggested Varieties and Planting Info	Family Interest Score (B)	square feet needed per person (C)	(D) = SF Needed (Adults x BxC)/10	Seeds, plants, bulbs etc. to plant per square foot (E)	Thin to # of plants per square foot	Seeds, plants, etc. Needed	Approx. days to harvest
plant 20 seeds per foot. Harvest thinnings with scissors. Leave one plant per foot and harvest a leaf at a time.								
SPRING PLANTING DATE	/							
Lettuce, Bibb	Bunte Forellenschuss Lettuce		2		20	1		45
Lettuce, Bibb - Purple	Pablo		2		20	1		45
Lettuce, Bibb - Your Variety			2		20	1		45
FALL PLANTING DATE	/							
Lettuce, Bibb	Bunte Forellenschuss Lettuce		2		20	1		45
Lettuce, Bibb - Purple	Pablo		2		20	1		45
Lettuce, Bibb - Your Variety			2		20	1		45

Lettuce, Bibb

Suggested Varieties and Planting Info	Family Interest Score (B)	square feet needed per person (C)	(D) = SF Needed (Adults x BxC)/10	Seeds, plants, bulbs etc. to plant per square foot (E)	Thin to # of plants per square foot	Seeds, plants, etc. Needed (DxE)	Approx. days to harvest
WINTER PLANTING DATE /							
Bunte Forellenschuss Lettuce		2		20	1		45
Lettuce, Bibb – Purple		2		20	1		45
Lettuce, Bibb – Your Variety		2		20	1		45

Lettuce – Buttercrunch Type - Grandpa Admire's Lettuce

George Admire was a Civil War veteran born in 1822. In 1977, 90-year-old Cloe Lowrey, Grandpa Admire's granddaughter, gave the seed to the Whealys in northern Missouri. Bronze-tinged leaf lettuce that forms large loose heads. Mild fine flavor, slow to bolt, tender longer than most, even in extreme heat. Butterhead.

plant 20 seeds per foot. Harvest thinnings with scissors. Leave one plant per foot and harvest a leaf at a time.

Lettuce, Buttercrunch

Suggested Varieties and Planting Info	Family Interest Score (B)	square feet needed per person (C)	(D) = SF Needed (Adults x BxC)/10	Seeds, plants, bulbs etc. to plant per square foot (E)	Thin to # of plants per square foot	Seeds, plants, etc. Needed (DxE)	Approx. days to harvest
SPRING PLANTING DATE /							
Lettuce, Leaf (Buttercrunch) Grandpa Admire's Lettuce		2		20	1		45
Lettuce, Leaf (Buttercrunch) - Your Variety		2		20	1		45

Lettuce, Buttercrunch	Suggested Varieties and Planting Info	Family Interest Score (B)	square feet needed per person (C)	(D) = SF Needed (Adults x BxC)/10	Seeds, plants, bulbs etc. to plant per square foot (E)	Thin to # of plants per square foot	Seeds, plants, etc. Needed	Approx. days to harvest
FALL PLANTING DATE	/							
Lettuce, Leaf (Buttercrunch)	Grandpa Admire's Lettuce		2		20	1		45
Lettuce, Leaf (Buttercrunch) - Your Variety			2		20	1		45
WINTER PLANTING DATE	/							
Lettuce, Leaf (Buttercrunch)	Grandpa Admire's Lettuce		2		20	1		45
Lettuce, Leaf (Buttercrunch) - Your Variety			2		20	1		45

Lettuce – Greenleaf Type - Amish Deer Tongue Lettuce

Amish variety valued for its ruggedness and heavy production. Thick solid compact plant. Sharply triangular green leaves with straight edges. Unique growth habit. Thin midrib, good texture. Pleasantly sharp flavor. Looseleaf.

Lettuce – Greenleaf Type - Australian Yellowleaf Lettuce

Australian heirloom with very tender texture. Unique color that is almost a neon chartreuse. Plants grow very large and are slow to bolt. Looseleaf.

Lettuce, Green Leaf

plant 20 seeds per foot. Harvest thinnings with scissors. Leave one plant per foot and harvest a leaf at a time.

Suggested Varieties and Planting Info	Family Interest Score (B)	square feet needed per person (C)	(D) = SF Needed (Adults x BxC)/10	Seeds, plants, bulbs etc. to plant per square foot (E)	Thin to # of plants per square foot	Seeds, plants, etc. Needed (DxE)	Approx. days to harvest
SPRING PLANTING DATE /							
Amish Deer Tongue Lettuce		2		20	1		45
Australian Yellowleaf Lettuce		2		20	1		45
Lettuce, Your Variety		2		20	1		45
FALL PLANTING DATE /							
Amish Deer Tongue Lettuce		2		20	1		45
Australian Yellowleaf Lettuce		2		20	1		45
Lettuce, Your Variety		2		20	1		45
WINTER PLANTING DATE /							
Amish Deer Tongue Lettuce		2		20	1		45
Australian Yellowleaf Lettuce		2		20	1		45
Lettuce, Your Variety		2		20	1		45

Lettuce - Mesclun Mix

Mesclun mix is any collection of salad greens grown all together, similar to what you might find in a fancy restaurant salad. Different mixes are available from different sources. Experiment with different combinations.

Lettuce, Mesclun Mix	Family Interest Score (B)	square feet needed per person (C)	(D) = SF Needed (Adults x BxC)/10	Seeds, plants, bulbs etc. to plant per square foot (E)	Thin to # of plants per square foot	Seeds, plants, etc. Needed (DxE)	Approx. days to harvest
Suggested Varieties and Planting Info							
plant 20 seeds per foot. Harvest thinnings with scissors. Leave one plant per foot and harvest a leaf at a time.							
SPRING PLANTING DATE							
Lettuce, Mesclun Mix	/						
Mesclun Mix		2		20	1		45
FALL PLANTING DATE							
Lettuce, Mesclun Mix	/						
Mesclun Mix		2		20	1		45
WINTER PLANTING DATE							
Lettuce, Mesclun Mix	/						
Mesclun Mix		2		20	1		45

Lettuce – Red Looseleaf Type - Red Velvet Lettuce

Red leaf lettuce is absolutely striking in a salad and this variety is the deepest red I've ever seen. Tops of leaves are solid reddish maroon, and the backs are green tinged with maroon. SSE is proud to have re-introduced this variety in 2002. Heads are slow to bolt, 6-8" tall and 10-12" wide. Pleasant, chewy texture. Looseleaf.

Lettuce, Red Leaf

plant 20 seeds per foot. Harvest thinnings with scissors. Leave one plant per foot and harvest a leaf at a time.

Suggested Varieties and Planting Info	Family Interest Score (B)	square feet needed per person (C)	(D) = SF Needed (Adults x BxC)/10	Seeds, plants, bulbs etc. to plant per square foot (E)	Thin to # of plants per square foot	Seeds, plants, etc. Needed (DxE)	Approx. days to harvest
SPRING PLANTING DATE /							
Lettuce, Leaf (Red Leaf)		2		20	1		45
Lettuce, Leaf (Red Leaf) - Your Variety		2		20	1		45
Lettuce, Your Variety		2		20	1		45
FALL PLANTING DATE /							
Lettuce, Leaf (Red Leaf)		2		20	1		45
Lettuce, Leaf (Red Leaf) - Your Variety		2		20	1		45
Lettuce, Your Variety		2		20	1		45
WINTER PLANTING DATE /							
Lettuce, Leaf (Red Leaf)		2		20	1		45
Lettuce, Leaf (Red Leaf) - Your Variety		2		20	1		45
Lettuce, Your Variety		2		20	1		45

Red Velvet Lettuce

Lettuce – Romaine Type - Crisp Mint Lettuce

No, this lettuce does NOT have a mint flavor. Compact heads grow almost straight up to a height of 10", excellent taste Unique, almost serrated leaves. A real standout.

plant 20 seeds per foot. Harvest thinnings with scissors. Leave one plant per foot and harvest a leaf at a time.

Lettuce, Romaine — Suggested Varieties and Planting Info	Family Interest Score (B)	square feet needed per person (C)	(D) = SF Needed (Adults x BxC)/10	Seeds, plants, bulbs etc. to plant per square foot (E)	Thin to # of plants per square foot	Seeds, plants, etc. Needed (DxE)	Approx. days to harvest
SPRING PLANTING DATE /							
Lettuce, Romaine — Crisp Mint Lettuce		2		20	1		45
Lettuce, Romaine - Your Variety		2		20	1		45
FALL PLANTING DATE /							
Lettuce, Romaine — Crisp Mint Lettuce		2		20	1		45
Lettuce, Romaine - Your Variety		2		20	1		45
WINTER PLANTING DATE /							
Lettuce, Romaine — Crisp Mint Lettuce		2		20	1		45
Lettuce, Romaine - Your Variety		2		20	1		45

Lima Beans

If your only experience with lima beans has been from frozen cardboard boxes, you're in for a treat. Pick the pods when the beans are plump, boil them in shallow water for a minute or two and add some butter! Harvest when the pods first start to bulge with the enlarged seeds. Pods must still be green, not yellowish.

Christmas Lima Bean

Produces beautiful large quarter-sized flat white seeds with maroon spots and swirls. Used as a green shell lima or dry. Rich flavor with heavy yields. Bears even during extreme heat. Dates back to the 1840s.

Lima Beans, Pole	Suggested Varieties and Planting Info	Family Interest Score (B)	square feet needed per person (C)	(D) = SF Needed (Adults x BxC)/10	Seeds, plants, bulbs etc. to plant per square foot (E)	Thin to # of plants per square foot	Seeds, plants, etc. Needed (DxE)	Approx. days to harvest
plant one seed every 4 inches along trellis	/							
SUMMER PLANTING DATE								
Lima Beans, Pole	Christmas Lima Bean		1		3	3		85
Lima Beans, Pole - Your Variety			1		3	3		85

Mustard Greens

Mustard greens are a quick-to-mature, easy-to-grow, cool-season vegetable for greens or salads. They are high in vitamins A and C. Harvest the leaves and leaf stems when they are 6 to 8 inches long; new leaves will provide a continuous harvest until they become strong in flavor and tough in texture from temperature extremes.

Mustard Greens

plant seeds 6 per square feet. Thin to 3 per square foot. Harvest the leaves and leaf stems when they are 6 to 8 inches long new leaves will provide a continuous harvest until they become strong in flavor and tough in texture from temperature extremes.

Suggested Varieties and Planting Info	Family Interest Score (B)	square feet needed per person (C)	(D) = SF Needed (Adults x BxC)/10	Seeds, plants, bulbs etc. to plant per square foot (E)	Thin to # of plants per square foot	Seeds, plants, etc. Needed (DxE)	Approx. days to harvest
SPRING PLANTING DATE							
Mustard Greens		2		6	3		35
FALL PLANTING DATE							
Mustard Greens		2		6	3		35
WINTER PLANTING DATE							
Mustard Greens		2		6	3		35

Onions

Onions are lots of fun to grow, especially if you start as spring onions, thin them as scallions, and leave the rest to "bulb out" into full grown onions. *See "Planting Thick and Thin."*

Ailsa Craig Onion

Introduced in 1887 by David Murray, gardener for the Marquis of Ailsa. Named after a small island off the coast of England that is round and solid rock. A cross between Danver's Yellow and Cranston's Excelsior, described as "Handsome, globe-shaped variety; large, solid, with small neck; straw color. An exhibition variety." Averages 2 pounds, excellent keeper.

Onions - Vidalia Type

Very popular for its mild, sweet flavor. Available locally as sets or bulbs only.

Onions - Bulbs	Family Interest Score (B)	square feet needed per person (C)	(D) = SF Needed (Adults x BxC)/10	Seeds, plants, bulbs etc. to plant per square foot (E)	Thin to # of plants per square foot	Seeds, plants, etc. Needed (DxE)	Approx. days to harvest
Suggested Varieties and Planting Info /							
place onion sets 4" apart at a rate of 16 per square foot, use thinnings as scallions and leave 9 plants to grow as bulbs.							
SPRING PLANTING DATE /							
Onions - Scallions/Spring Onions — Ailsa Craig Onion		1		16	9		70
Onions - Bulbs — Vidalia Type		1		16	9		70
Onions - Bulbs - Your Variety		1		16	9		70
FALL PLANTING DATE /							
Onions - Scallions/Spring Onions — Ailsa Craig Onion		1		16	9		70
Onions - Bulbs — Vidalia Type		1		16	9		70
Onions - Bulbs - Your Variety		1		16	9		70

Pak Choy

Pak Choy, also called "**Chinese Cabbage,**" is one of the most popular vegetables grown and sold in the supermarkets on the West Coast and Orient. This fast-growing vegetable has tender green leaves and crispy green petioles. Green Baby Pok Choy has become the most used vegetables in various Oriental dishes due to its excellent flavor, texture and size.

Peas

In my opinion, fresh peas are the reason to have a home garden. Their flavor is like candy. Harvest "shelling" peas when the pods are well rounded. "Sugar snap" peas are dual purpose. You can pick them when the peas have plumped out a bit and cook them whole or use them in salads, or you can wait until the pods are fuller and treat them as shelling peas. Snow peas are picked while the pods are still thin and cooked whole. Most often used in Chinese dishes, they're great raw in salads! Leave a few pods on the vine to dry and you'll have seeds for next year for your kids to plant.

Peas - Shelling - Sutton's Harbinger Pea

Introduced in England in 1898 and received an Award of Merit from the Royal Horticultural Society in 1901. Crossed the Atlantic in 1903. Very early, heavy-cropping variety. Excellent quality eating pea. Plants are 28-32" tall. Shelling pea. Shelling Peas are grown to maturity and the pods are unzipped to remove the peas. Careful, you may eat more of them raw than end up in your bowl! Boil or steam for a few minutes and you'll have a treat.

Peas – Sugar Snap Type - Amish Snap Pea

Superb snap pea that was being grown in the Amish community long before present snap pea types. Vines grow 5-6' tall and are heavy producers of 2" pods. Yields over a 6-week period if kept picked. Delicate and sweet even when the seeds develop. Curved sickle-shaped pods.

Peas – Snow Type - Dwarf Gray Sugar Pea

Introduced in 1892 by D. M. Ferry & Company. Broad pale-green 3-4" pods are stringless, fiber-free and well suited for steaming or used in stir-fry. Vines are 24-30" and do not require staking, beautiful purple blossoms.

Peas, Pole

plant one seed every 3 inches along trellis

Suggested Varieties and Planting Info	Family Interest Score (B)	square feet needed per person (C)	(D) = SF Needed (Adults x BxC)/10	Seeds, plants, bulbs etc. to plant per square foot (E)	Thin to # of plants per square foot	Seeds, plants, etc. Needed (DxE)	Approx. days to harvest
SPRING PLANTING DATE /							
Peas, Pole, Shelling — Sutton's Harbinger Pea		1		4	4		65
Peas, Pole, Snow — Dwarf Gray Sugar Pea		1		4	4		65
Peas, Pole, Sugar Snap		1		4	4		65
Peas - Your Variety		1		4	4		65
FALL PLANTING DATE /							
Peas, Pole, Shelling — Sutton's Harbinger Pea		1		4	4		65
Peas, Pole, Snow — Dwarf Gray Sugar Pea		1		4	4		65
Peas, Pole, Sugar Snap		1		4	4		65
Peas - Your Variety		1		4	4		65
WINTER PLANTING DATE /							
Peas, Pole, Shelling — Sutton's Harbinger Pea		1		4	4		65
Peas, Pole, Snow — Dwarf Gray Sugar Pea		1		4	4		65
Peas, Pole, Sugar Snap		1		4	4		65
Peas - Your Variety		1		4	4		65

Peppers

The variety of peppers is astounding, from mildly spicy to rocket hot. They are best grown from transplants. It's good to ask around and experiment with single plants of different varieties until you come up with some favorites.

Hot Peppers

Harvest hot peppers with a sharp knife when the fruits are firm, crisp, and full size. Allow hot peppers to attain their bright red color and full flavor while attached to the vine, then cut them and hang them to dry.

Peppers - Sweet Banana peppers

The banana pepper is a very productive plant producing banana-shaped fruits that change from pale to deep yellow or orange as they mature. They are sweet, long, tapered, yellow and banana-shaped, hence the name. Sweet banana peppers may be fried or sautéed, used raw on relish platters, in salads, sandwiches or stuffed.

Peppers - Sweet Bell Type

Sweet peppers are sliced for salads or can be stuffed. As they ripen on the plant they change color and become sweeter.

Buran Pepper

Extremely sweet and productive Polish heirloom. Great flavor! Medium-sized plants grow 18-24" tall. Fruits are 3-lobed and measure 4" long by 3" at the shoulders. Fruits are almost equally sweet when either green or red.

Orange Bell Pepper

Seed Savers says "this is the best tasting orange bell we have grown at Heritage Farm. Blocky 4 by 3½" fruits are 3-4 lobed, extremely thick-fleshed with excellent sweet flavor, and heavy yields. Almost entirely four-lobed fruits. Original seed source was SSE member Alex Heklar in 1989. Brought to our attention by Dr. Jeff Nekola at University of Wisconsin at Green Bay, where this variety is very popular each spring at their plant sale." 60 days from transplant for green peppers, 90 days for orange.

Peppers, (use transplants)	Suggested Varieties and Planting Info	Family Interest Score (B)	square feet needed per person (C)	(D) = SF Needed (Adults x BxC)/10	Seeds, plants, bulbs etc. to plant per square foot (E)	Thin to # of plants per square foot	Seeds, plants, etc. Needed (DxE)	Approx. days to harvest
place transplants 20" apart	/							
SUMMER PLANTING DATE								
Peppers, hot	Various Varieties		0.5		0.7	0.7		80
Peppers, sweet banana	Sweet Banana		0.5		0.7	0.7		80
Peppers, sweet bell – Orange	Orange Bell Pepper		0.5		0.7	0.7		80
Peppers, sweet bell – Red	Buran Pepper		0.5		0.7	0.7		80
Peppers - Your Variety			0.5		0.7	0.7		80
Peppers - Your Variety			0.5		0.7	0.7		80

Potatoes

Not a very efficient crop because they take up a bit of room, but there are so many unique varieties, it's worth trying in your garden. Plant early in the spring for "new potatoes" before the heat of summer, and in the fall for larger tubers to be harvested in early spring. When you see flowers starting to form, that means you can sneak out a few tender potatoes by digging around the edges! Harvest the tubers when the plants begin to dry and die down. Store them in a cool, high-humidity location with good ventilation, such as the basement or crawl space to the house. Avoid exposing the them to light. Greening, which denotes the presence of dangerous alkaloids, will occur even with small amounts of light.

All Red Potato - Pink Flesh

(a.k.a. **Cranberry Red**) Red skin with delicate pale pink flesh. Low starch content makes this variety a good boiling potato for salads or any dish that requires potatoes to retain their shape. Considered the best producing red-fleshed, red-skinned variety. Introduced to SSE members by Robert Lobitz in 1984. Consistently a good producer, regardless of the weather conditions.

German Butterball Potato - Yellow Flesh

First place winner in Rodale's Organic Gardening "Taste Off." A good choice for roasting, frying and mashed potatoes. Russeted skin and buttery yellow flesh. One of our favorite all-purpose potatoes. Excellent for long-term storage.

Purple Viking Potato - White Flesh

Quickly gaining the reputation of a great tasting, slightly sweet, general purpose potato. A choice variety for any preparation, snow-white flesh is excellent for mashing. Average tubers are 3½ - 4" in diameter, but in a good year it can produce even larger tubers. Excellent storage qualities.

Potatoes	Suggested Varieties and Planting Info	Family Interest Score (B)	square feet needed per person (C)	(D) = SF Needed (Adults x BxC)/10	Seeds, plants, bulbs etc. to plant per square foot (E)	Thin to # of plants per square foot	Seeds, plants, etc. Needed (DxE)	Approx. days to harvest
plant seed potatoes 5" deep and 8" apart	/							
SPRING PLANTING DATE	/							
Potatoes - Pink	All Red Potato - Pink Flesh		1		2	2		100
Potatoes - White - Purple Skin	Purple Viking Potato - White Flesh		1		2	2		100
Potatoes - Yellow			1		2	2		100
Potatoes - Your Variety			1		2	2		100
FALL PLANTING DATE	/							
Potatoes - Pink	All Red Potato - Pink Flesh		1		2	2		100
Potatoes - White - Purple Skin	Purple Viking Potato - White Flesh		1		2	2		100
Potatoes - Yellow			1		2	2		100
Potatoes - Your Variety			1		2	2		100

Raspberries

Raspberries are a bramble and grow in your native soil. They prefer good sun and can go anywhere on your property as a perennial. Available locally as transplants or through mail order as bare root plants. Plant two feet apart. One plant per person. Plant in the fall or spring. You will need to plan for a simple wire trellis to support the vines.

Radishes

Harvest when the roots are 1/2 to 1 1/2 inches in diameter. They grow fast, often ready for harvest in three weeks. The shoulders of radish roots often appear through the soil surface when they are mature. If left in the ground too long, they can become tough and woody.

Radish - Spicy - French Breakfast Radish

Oblong and blunt, rose-scarlet with a white tip. Flesh is white and crisp, mildly pungent flavor, top quality. Sow in the spring or fall, pick when small. A garden standard since the 1880s.

Radishes - Helios Radish – Sweet

Named for the Greek God of the sun. Pale yellow, sweet spring radish with white flesh. Most likely the same variety described in Vilmorin's The Vegetable Garden (1885) as "Small Early Yellow Turnip Radish."

Radishes - Philadelphia White Box Radish - Sweet

Historic radish variety from the 1890s, listed by D. Landreth Seed Company (the oldest seed house in the U.S., established in 1784) in 1938 as a good variety for open cultivation or forcing in boxes. Nice and mild, sow in early spring or early fall.

Radishes - Plum Purple Radish – Sweet

Unique deep purple round roots. Firm, white flesh, sweet and mild all season, hardy and adaptable, never pithy. Exceptional variety for the novelty market and home gardener.

Radishes

plant seed at a rate of 9 per square foot. Harvest when the roots are 1/2 to 1 1/2 inches in diameter.

Suggested Varieties and Planting Info	Family Interest Score (B)	square feet needed per person (C)	(D) = SF Needed (Adults x BxC)/10	Seeds, plants, bulbs etc. to plant per square foot (E)	Thin to # of plants per square foot	Seeds, plants, etc. Needed (DxE)	Approx. days to harvest
SPRING PLANTING DATE /							
Radishes - Hot French Breakfast Radish		1		9	9		25
Radishes - Mild - Yellow Helios Radish - Sweet		1		9	9		25
Radishes - Mild - White Philadelphia White Box		1		9	9		25
Radishes - Mild - Purple Plum Purple Radish		1		9	9		25
Radishes - Your Variety		1		9	9		25
Radishes - Your Variety		1		9	9		25
FALL PLANTING DATE /							
Radishes - Hot French Breakfast Radish		1		9	9		25
Radishes - Mild - Yellow Helios Radish - Sweet		1		9	9		25
Radishes - Mild - White Philadelphia White Box		1		9	9		25
Radishes - Mild - Purple Plum Purple Radish		1		9	9		25
Radishes - Your Variety		1		9	9		25
Radishes - Your Variety		1		9	9		25
WINTER PLANTING DATE /							
Radishes - Hot French Breakfast Radish		1		9	9		25
Radishes - Mild - Yellow Helios Radish - Sweet		1		9	9		25
Radishes - Mild - White Philadelphia White Box		1		9	9		25
Radishes - Mild - Purple Plum Purple Radish		1		9	9		25
Radishes - Your Variety		1		9	9		25
Radishes - Your Variety		1		9	9		25

Rhubarb

Rhubarb is a spring-harvested perennial that ranges in color from green to bright red. Traditionally, it played a significant role in the American diet. A rhubarb plant can stay in production for over a decade. It is a member of the Buckwheat family and therefore related to sorrel and dock. It has a rich but tart flavor. Some folks like to eat it raw where others mix it with some type of sweetener and make rhubarb pie. The leaf stalks are the edible portion. The leaves are actually poisonous, so be careful around young children.

Rhubarb is a cool weather crop and is difficult to grow in warm climates. It needs rich, well-drained soil, and we place it on the shady side of our asparagus ferns where it will get relief from some of the summer heat. It's grown from a root or crown and it sometimes takes several tries to get your crop established. Plant in the fall or early spring.

Rhubarb (rhizomes)	Suggested Varieties and Planting Info	Family In-terest Score (B)	square feet needed per person (C)	(D) = SF Needed (Adults x BxC)/10	Seeds, plants, bulbs etc. to plant per square foot (E)	Thin to # of plants per square foot	Seeds, plants, etc. Needed (DxE)	Approx. days to harvest
plant rhizome in center of desired location in coolest part of the garden.								
SPRING PLANTING DATE								
Rhubarb	Rhubarb Crowns		0.7		1	1		annual
FALL PLANTING DATE								
Rhubarb	Rhubarb Crowns		0.7		1	1		annual
WINTER PLANTING DATE								
Rhubarb	Rhubarb Crowns		0.7		1	1		annual

Shallots

Shallots are often thought to be another variety of onion, but they are actually a species of their own. They grow in clusters, where separate bulbs are attached at the base and by loose skins. The shallot has a tapered shape and a fine-textured, coppery skin, which differentiates it from onions.

Shallots have a mild taste that combines the flavor of a sweet onion with a touch of garlic. They're expensive in the stores, so are a great crop for the back yard garden. Sometimes it's easier to find small shallots at the grocery store and plant those.

plant shallot cloves root side down at a rate of 9 per square foot

Shallots (cloves)	Suggested Varieties and Planting Info	Family Interest Score (B)	square feet needed per person (C)	(D) = SF Needed (Adults x BxC)/10	Seeds, plants, bulbs etc. to plant per square foot (E)	Thin to # of plants per square foot	Seeds, plants, etc. Needed (DxE)	Approx. days to harvest
SPRING PLANTING DATE	/							
Shallots			1		9	9		120
FALL PLANTING DATE	/							
Shallots			1		9	9		120
WINTER PLANTING DATE	/							
Shallots			1		9	9		120

Soy Beans – Edamame
Shirofumi Soybean

This variety is gaining popularity as the best green soybean available. Large pale-green seeds, extremely productive. An SSE member reported that one 100' row produced 38 pounds of unshelled pods! For a better harvest, make sure you get a climbing, pole variety instead of a bush variety.

Soy Beans - Edamame	Suggested Varieties and Planting Info	Family Interest Score (B)	square feet needed per person (C)	(D) = SF Needed (Adults x BxC)/10	Seeds, plants, bulbs etc. to plant per square foot (E)	Thin to # of plants per square foot	Seeds, plants, etc. Needed (DxE)	Approx. days to harvest
plant one seed every 3 inches along trellis								
SPRING PLANTING DATE								
Soy Beans - Edamame	Shirofumi Soybean		1		4	4		85

Spinach

Spinach can be hard to get started. It needs temperatures between 40° and 60° for best germination. When 6 or more leaves have been formed, harvest by cutting all the leaves off at the base of the plant when they are 4 to 6 inches long. New leaves will grow, providing additional harvests. *See "Planting Thick and Thin."*

Monnopa Spinach

Claimed to be the sweetest of all spinach. A round-leafed variety with very little oxalic acid. High in vitamins A, C and E. Low acid improves the absorption of calcium and other minerals.

Spinach

plant seeds at a rate of 12 per square foot and thin to 6 per foot. Harvest by cutting all the leaves off at the base of the plant when there are at least six leaves that are 4 to 6 inches long. New leaves will grow, providing additional harvests.

Suggested Varieties and Planting Info	Family Interest Score (B)	square feet needed per person (C)	(D) = SF Needed (Adults x BxC)/10	Seeds, plants, bulbs etc. to plant per square foot (E)	Thin to # of plants per square foot	Seeds, plants, etc. Needed (DxE)	Approx. days to harvest
SPRING PLANTING DATE /							
Spinach Monnopa Spinach		2		12	6		55
Spinach - Your Variety		2		12	6		55
FALL PLANTING DATE /							
Spinach Monnopa Spinach		2		12	6		55
Spinach - Your Variety		2		12	6		55
WINTER PLANTING DATE /							
Spinach Monnopa Spinach		2		12	6		55
Spinach - Your Variety		2		12	6		55

Spinach – SUMMER VARIETY! - New Zealand Spinach

Not a true spinach, but similar in flavor and usage. GROWS DURING SUMMER SEASON. Large strong spreading plants branch freely. Small brittle fleshy green leaves, great for fresh summer greens. Thrives in hot weather, will not bolt or get bitter. Best when 4" tips of branches are picked all summer and fall. Good disease and insect resistance. New Zealand native brought to Europe by Captain Cook in the 1770s. Good source of vitamin C. Seeds are slow to germinate, so be patient.

Summer Spinach	Suggested Varieties and Planting Info	Family Interest Score (B)	square feet needed per person (C)	(D) = SF Needed (Adults x BxC)/10	Seeds, plants, bulbs etc. to plant per square foot (E)	Thin to # of plants per square foot	Seeds, plants, etc. Needed (DxE)	Approx. days to harvest
SUMMER PLANTING DATE	/							
Summer Spinach	New Zealand		2		9	6		60

Squash

Very popular in home gardens, squash grow rapidly and can be very productive. Harvest when the fruit is soft, tender, and 6 to 8 inches long (3 to 4 inches across for patty pans). The skin color often changes to a dark, glossy green or yellow, depending on variety. Pick every two or three days to encourage production. NOTE: All squash are affected by squash vine borers. *For more info on what they are and how to deal with them, read the article in the Appendix.* Other problems... *Poor fruit set of vine crops?* -- Poor pollination is the problem. Squash, cucumbers, and other vine crops produce both male and female blossoms. It is normal for vine crops to produce 10 or more male blossoms before female blossoms are formed. The male blossoms will drop without any food production. Bees are needed to transfer the pollen from male to female blossoms.

Squash - Patty Pan Type (Pattison panache jaune et vert Squash)
Sent to SSE by French member Bruno Defay. Bowl-shaped bush scallop with good yields of yellowish cream fruits with bands of green. Good eating qualities when young and a very nice, rock-hard ornamental when mature.

Squash - Yellow - Summer Crookneck Squash
Semi-open bush plants produce extended heavy crops of smooth light yellow fruits with curved necks, bumped developed after edible stage. Best eaten when 5-6" long. Creamy-white sweet mild flesh has excellent flavor. Keep picked clean to enjoy all season.

Squash - Zucchini - Black Beauty Zucchini Squash

The standard summer squash. Compact spiny everbearing bush with dark greenish-black skinned fruits. Long, cylindrical fruits are best eaten when 6-8" long. Excellent variety for freezing.

Squash	Family Interest Score (B)	square feet needed per person (C)	(D) = SF Needed (Adults x BxC)/10	Seeds, plants, bulbs etc. to plant per square foot (E)	Thin to # of plants per square foot	Seeds, plants, etc. Needed	Approx. days to harvest
plant three seeds 1" apart in center of desired location, thin to one strong plant. Pick every two or three days to encourage production.							
SPRING PLANTING DATE /							
Squash – Patty Pan Pattison panache jaune et vert Squash		1		0.5	0.5		55
Squash – Yellow Summer Crookneck Squash		1		0.5	0.5		55
Squash – Zucchini		1		0.5	0.5		55
Squash – Your Variety		1		0.5	0.5		55

Strawberries

Strawberries are another perennial in the home garden and require rich, well-drained soil. They take a bit of maintenance, mostly clipping off runners that will overtake the rest of your garden. Transplants can sometimes be hard to get started. If only half of them take hold, place the ends of runners in the bare spots to fill them in. Strawberries can bear fruit at different times, all in the spring ("spring bearing"), all in the early fall ("fall bearing"), part spring and fall ("everbearing"), and throughout the season ("day neutral"). We use a day neutral variety called "Tribute" for an ongoing harvest, but you can try different options. Strawberries can also be grown in large pots, but they're hard to keep watered. Plant in fall or early spring

Strawberries (plants) Suggested Varieties and Planting Info	Family Interest Score (B)	square feet needed per person (C)	(D) = SF Needed (Adults x BxC)/10	Seeds, plants, bulbs etc. to plant per square foot (E)	Thin to # of plants per square foot	Seeds, plants, etc. Needed (DxE)	Approx. days to harvest
Plant 4 bare root plants per square foot. Spread roots widely onto an earth cone and cover so that the crowns are 1/2" above the soil line. Mulch with fine pine nuggets.							
SPRING PLANTING DATE /							
strawberries (plants) Tribute		2		4	4		annual
strawberries - Your Variety		2		4	4		annual
FALL PLANTING DATE /							
strawberries (plants) Tribute		2		4	4		annual
strawberries - Your Variety		2		4	4		annual

Sweet Potatoes - Yellow - Nancy Halls

Sweet potatoes are very nutritious, but orange and red varieties are very common and inexpensive. We use a variety called Nancy Halls, which has yellow flesh with a unique buttery, nutty flavor. Planted as transplants, they are vines that will quickly take over your whole garden. Weave them up a trellis as they grow.

Harvest the roots when they are large enough for use before frost. Avoid bruising or scratching during handling. (*Damaged sweet potatoes rot easily in storage.*) Ideal storage conditions are a temperature of 55° and a relative humidity of 85%. The basement or crawl space of a house may suffice. *See the article on Sweet Potatoes in the Appendix.*

Sweet Potatoes (slips)	Suggested Varieties and Planting Info	Family Interest Score (B)	square feet needed per person (C)	(D) = SF Needed (Adults x BxC)/10	Seeds, plants, bulbs etc. to plant per square foot (E)	Thin to # of plants per square foot	Seeds, plants, etc. Needed (DxE)	Approx. days to harvest
plant slips 5" apart at a rate of 4 per square foot within 2' of trellis. Train vines up trellis as they grow.								
SUMMER PLANTING DATE /								
Sweet Potatoes - Yellow	Yellow - Nancy Halls		2		4	4		100

Swiss Chard

Chard is a type of beet that has been developed for its greens instead of its roots. Break off the developed outer leaves 1 inch above the soil. New leaves will grow, providing a continuous harvest without injuring the plant.

Swiss Chard - Five Color Silverbeet

This variety offers a spectacular range of five neon colors throughout the entire season. Put it in the front of your garden where everyone can see it!

Swiss chard	Suggested Varieties and Planting Info	Family Interest Score (B)	square feet needed per person (C)	(D) = SF Needed (Adults x BxC)/10	Seeds, plants, bulbs etc. to plant per square foot (E)	Thin to # of plants per square foot	Seeds, plants, etc. Needed (DxE)	Approx. days to harvest
SPRING PLANTING DATE /								
Swiss chard	Five Color Silverbeet		2		4	2		65
FALL PLANTING DATE /								
Swiss chard	Five Color Silverbeet		2		4	2		65

Tomatoes

Easily the most popular vegetable in today's gardens. They're easy to get started as transplants and there are scores of excellent varieties to try. They can be divided into three general groups based on fruit size, beefsteak, roma and cherry/grape. Tomatoes suffer from all sorts of problems, so please see *the article on growing tomatoes in the Appendix*. Also find tips on how to make your tomatoes as productive as possible in a limited space. Avoid bush type (determinate) plants in favor of climbing (indeterminate) varieties.

Tomatoes – Beefsteak type

Beefsteak tomatoes are among the most popular. Also called "slicing tomatoes," they're meant to be used fresh in salads or sandwiches. Their flesh is usually too watery to use in soups or sauces. I recommend heirloom varieties, but there are many modern ones to try as well.

Brandywine (Sudduth's Strain)

Brandywine first appeared in the 1889 catalog of Johnson & Stokes of Philadelphia and by 1902 was also offered by four additional seed companies, but soon disappeared from all commercial catalogs. Our best selling tomato and one of the best tasting tomatoes available to gardeners today. The seed of this strain was obtained by tomato collector Ben Quisenberry of Big Tomato Gardens in 1980 from Dorris Sudduth Hill whose family grew them for 80 years. Large Pink beefsteak fruits to 2 pounds. Incredibly rich, delightfully intense tomato flavor.

Cherokee Purple Tomato

Introduced to other SSE members by North Carolina member Craig LeHoullier in 1991, seed obtained from J. D. Green. Unique dusty rose color. Flavor rivals Brandywine, extremely sweet. Productive plants produce large crops of 12 oz. fruits.

German Pink
One of the two original Bavarian varieties that started Seed Savers. Potato-leaf plants produce large 1-2 pound meaty fruits with few seeds, very little cracking or blossom scars. Full sweet flavor. Excellent for canning and freezing. Dale Ott, Babtist Ott's son, is still growing this variety today in Festina, Iowa. In a typical season Dale will grow 30 plants and harvest 400 pounds of tomatoes for local customers.

Gold Medal
Listed on Ben Quisenberry's 1976 seed list as, "Large, yellow, streaked red; firm and smooth. Very little acid. The sweetest tomato you ever tasted. The yellow with streaks and blotches of red makes them very attractive and a gourmet's joy when sliced."

Tomatoes, Beef-steak (plants)	**Suggested Varieties and Planting Info**	**Family Interest Score (B)**	**square feet needed per person (C)**	**(D) = SF Needed (Adults x BxC)/10**	**Seeds, plants, bulbs etc. to plant per square foot (E)**	**Thin to # of plants per square foot**	**Seeds, plants, etc. Needed (DxE)**	**Approx. days to harvest**
plant transplants deeply 30" apart.								
SUMMER PLANTING DATE	/							
Tomatoes, Beefsteak	Brandywine (Sudduth's Strain)		0.4		0.5	0.5		80
Tomatoes, Beefsteak	Cherokee Purple Tomato		0.4		0.5	0.5		80
Tomatoes, Beefsteak	German Pink		0.4		0.5	0.5		80
Tomatoes, Beefsteak - Gold	Gold Medal		0.4		0.5	0.5		80
Tomatoes - Your Variety			0.4		0.5	0.5		80
Tomatoes - Your Variety			0.4		0.5	0.5		80

Tomatoes – Paste/Roma Type

Roma tomatoes, also called paste tomatoes, are often used in soups, sauces and stews because of their firmer flesh and lower water content.

Tomatoes – Paste/Roma Type - Speckled Roman

Developed by SSE member John Swenson as a result of a stabilized cross of Antique Roman and Banana Legs. Gorgeous 3" wide by 5" long fruits with jagged orange and yellow stripes. Meaty, great tomato taste, ideal for processing. Very productive, few seeds. Still throws an occasional yellow striped fruit.

Tomatoes, Roma	Family Interest Score (B)	square feet needed per person (C)	(D) = SF Needed (Adults x BxC)/10	Seeds, plants, bulbs etc. to plant per square foot (E)	Thin to # of plants per square foot	Seeds, plants, etc. Needed (DxE)	Approx. days to harvest
Speckled Roman							
SUMMER PLANTING DATE							
Tomatoes - Your Variety	0	0.4		0.5	0.5		80
strawberries - Your Variety		0.4		0.5	0.5		annual

Tomatoes - Cherry Type

Very productive plants. I rarely recommend more than one plant per family, since they produce so many tiny tomatoes that they're hard to keep harvested. Don't let any tomatoes fall and rot on the ground or you'll have tomatoes "volunteering" next year like crazy.

Tomatoes - Cherry Type - Mexico Midget

Very prolific plants continue producing throughout the entire growing season. Round ½" fruits give an incredible flash of rich tomato flavor, great for salads or selling in pints.

Sun Gold Yellow

They have a sweet flavor and really stand out in a salad. Very productive.

Tomatoes, Cherry	Suggested Varieties and Planting Info	Family Interest Score (B)	square feet needed per person (C)	(D) = SF Needed (Adults x BxC)/10	Seeds, plants, bulbs etc. to plant per square foot (E)	Thin to # of plants per square foot	Seeds, plants, etc. Needed (DxE)	Approx. days to harvest
plant transplants deeply 30" apart.	/							
SUMMER PLANTING DATE								
Tomatoes, Cherry - Red	Mexico Midget		0.3		0.5	0.5		80
Tomatoes, Cherry - Yellow	Sun Gold		0.3		0.5	0.5		80
Tomatoes - Your Variety			0.3		0.5	0.5		80

Turnips

Very similar to rutabagas, harvest the roots when they are 2 to 3 inches in diameter but before heavy frosts occur in the fall. The tops may be used as greens when the leaves are 3 to 5 inches long.

Turnips - Purple Top White Globe Turnip

Widely used by home gardeners and market growers since before 1880. Uniform 6" smooth white globes are best for eating when 3-4" in diameter. Sweet mild fine-grained white flesh. Excellent quality, stores extremely well.

plant seeds 4 per square feet. Thin to 2 per square foot. Harvest the roots when they are 2 to 3 inches in diameter.

Turnips	Suggested Varieties and Planting Info	Family Interest Score (B)	square feet needed per person (C)	(D) = SF Needed (Adults x BxC)/10	Seeds, plants, bulbs etc. to plant per square foot (E)	Thin to # of plants per square foot	Seeds, plants, etc. Needed (DxE)	Approx. days to harvest
SPRING PLANTING DATE	/							
Turnips	Purple Top White Globe	2	2		4	2		70
FALL PLANTING DATE	/							
Turnips	Purple Top White Globe	2	2		4	2		70
WINTER PLANTING DATE	/							
Turnips	Purple Top White Globe	2	2		4	2		70

GARDEN PLANNER - SPRING

PLANTING DATE _____ / _____

Crop Name	Plant Variety	NUMBER OF FAMILY MEMBERS (A)						
		Family Interest Score (B)	square feet needed per person (C)	(D) = SF Needed (Adults x BxC) / 10	Seeds, plants, bulbs etc. to plant per square foot (E)	Thin to # of plants per square foot	Seeds, plants, etc. Needed (DxE)	Approx. days to harvest

GARDEN PLANNER - SUMMER

Crop Name	Plant Variety	Family Interest Score (B)	square feet needed per person (C)	(D) = SF Needed (Adults x BxC)/10	Seeds, plants, bulbs etc. to plant per square foot (E)	Thin to # of plants per square foot	Seeds, plants, etc. Needed (DxE)	Approx. days to harvest

PLANTING DATE   /

NUMBER OF FAMILY MEMBERS (A)

GARDEN PLANNER - FALL

PLANTING DATE ___/___

Crop Name	Plant Variety	NUMBER OF FAMILY MEMBERS (A)							
		Family Interest Score (B)	square feet needed per person (C)	(D) = SF Needed (Adults x BxC)/10	Seeds, plants, bulbs etc. to plant per square foot (E)	Thin to # of plants per square foot	Seeds, plants, etc. Needed (DxE)	Approx. days to harvest

GARDEN PLANNER - WINTER

	PLANTING DATE /	NUMBER OF FAMILY MEMBERS (A)					
Crop Name	Plant Variety	Family Interest Score (B)	square feet needed per person (C)	(D) = SF Needed (Adults x BxC)/10	Seeds, plants, bulbs etc. to plant per square foot (E)	Thin to # of plants per square foot	Seeds, plants, etc. Needed (DxE)	Approx. days to harvest

Garden Planning with Spare Change!

Now that you have your plant list for each season, you know how many square feet you need for your garden because you've added it all up.

Hopefully, the totals for your cool season and summer crops are about the same size. If not, you might want to add or subtract to even things out.

RULE OF THUMB: You should be able to feed a family of four with a garden of 40 to 60 square feet. Any more than that and you're probably biting off more than you can chew!

Here are a few tricks to make laying out your garden easier...

PLANT SIZE CHART

SQUASH ZUCCHINI

TOMATO POTATO

EGGPLANT PEPPER

ONE SQUARE FOOT

BROCCOLI

Copy or rip out the Garden Layout page (next page). Take your Garden Planner list for the summer season and start arranging crops as follows... (*USE PENCIL!*)

1 Trellis/climbing plants first. These go in a row along the base of your trellis. So if you have a nine foot bed and you have six feet of beans and three feet of cucumbers, you're good to go!

2 Next, arrange your larger plants - squash, peppers, tomatoes, etc. If you have 40¢ you can make it very easy. Just use a quarter for each squash plant, a nickel for tomatoes and potatoes, and a dime for eggplant and peppers. Broccoli needs exactly one square foot, so you won't need a coin for that. Just move things around until you have a plan that makes sense. Trace around each coin and you'll have the exact size circle you need for each plant. *NOTE: There are no large cool-season crops.*

List your permanent crops below. They grow elsewhere in your landscape.

	Number of Plants Needed
Blackberries	
Blueberries	
Raspberries	

Garden Layout, Spring 20___

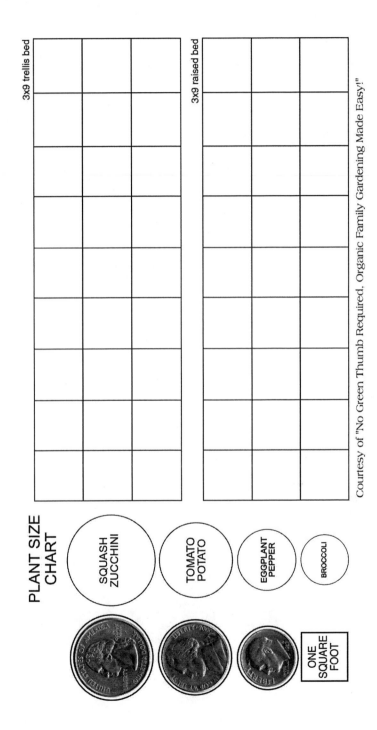

3x9 trellis bed

3x9 raised bed

PLANT SIZE CHART

SQUASH ZUCCHINI

TOMATO POTATO

EGGPLANT PEPPER

BROCCOLI

ONE SQUARE FOOT

Courtesy of "No Green Thumb Required, Organic Family Gardening Made Easy!"

Garden Layout, Summer 20___

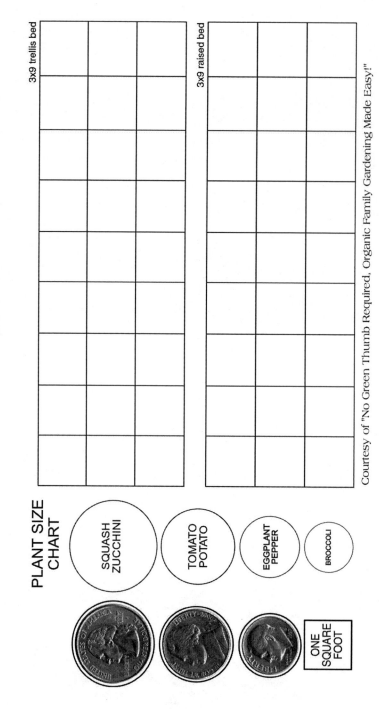

Courtesy of "No Green Thumb Required, Organic Family Gardening Made Easy!"

Garden Layout, Spring 20___

3x9 trellis bed

3x9 raised bed

PLANT SIZE CHART

SQUASH ZUCCHINI

TOMATO POTATO

EGGPLANT PEPPER

BROCCOLI

ONE SQUARE FOOT

Courtesy of "No Green Thumb Required, Organic Family Gardening Made Easy!"

Garden Layout, Summer 20__

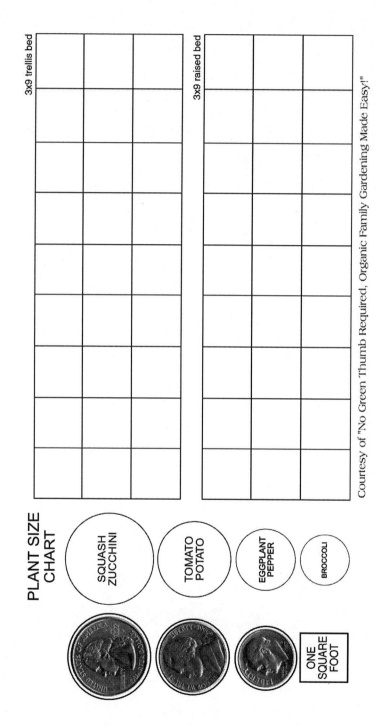

3x9 trellis bed

3x9 raised bed

Courtesy of "No Green Thumb Required, Organic Family Gardening Made Easy!"

PLANT SIZE CHART

SQUASH ZUCCHINI

TOMATO POTATO

EGGPLANT PEPPER

BROCCOLI

ONE SQUARE FOOT

The Smiths' Instant Organic Garden

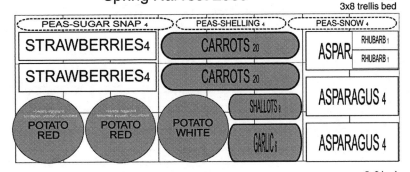

Spring Harvest 2009

3x8 trellis bed

PEAS-SUGAR SNAP 4	PEAS-SHELLING 4	PEAS-SNOW 4
STRAWBERRIES4	CARROTS 20	ASPAR / RHUBARB 1 / RHUBARB 1
STRAWBERRIES4	CARROTS 20	
POTATO RED / POTATO RED	POTATO WHITE / SHALLOTS 8	ASPARAGUS 4
	GARLIC 6	ASPARAGUS 4

3x8 bed

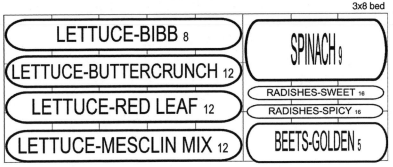

LETTUCE-BIBB 8	SPINACH 9
LETTUCE-BUTTERCRUNCH 12	
LETTUCE-RED LEAF 12	RADISHES-SWEET 16
	RADISHES-SPICY 16
LETTUCE-MESCLIN MIX 12	BEETS-GOLDEN 5

www.instantorganicgarden.com 704-364-1784 Instant Organic Garden - Plant-a-Gram™

The Smiths' Instant Organic Garden

Summer Harvest 2009

3x8 trellis bed

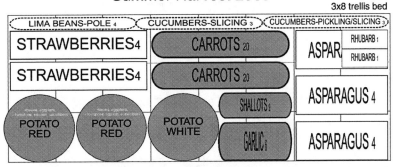

LIMA BEANS-POLE 4	CUCUMBERS-SLICING 3	CUCUMBERS-PICKLING/SLICING 3
STRAWBERRIES4	CARROTS 20	ASPAR / RHUBARB 1 / RHUBARB 1
STRAWBERRIES4	CARROTS 20	
POTATO RED / POTATO RED	POTATO WHITE / SHALLOTS 8	ASPARAGUS 4
	GARLIC 6	ASPARAGUS 4

PLANT CORN AS LIVE TRELLIS   3x8 bed

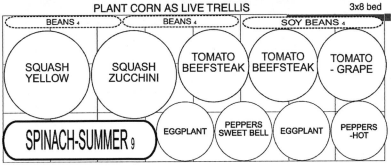

BEANS 4	BEANS 4	SOY BEANS 4
SQUASH YELLOW	SQUASH ZUCCHINI	TOMATO BEEFSTEAK	TOMATO BEEFSTEAK	TOMATO - GRAPE
SPINACH-SUMMER 9	EGGPLANT	PEPPERS SWEET BELL	EGGPLANT	PEPPERS -HOT

www.instantorganicgarden.com 704-364-1784 Instant Organic Garden - Plant-a-Gram™

Sample Instant Organic Garden
Spring Harvest 2009

2x8 trellis bed

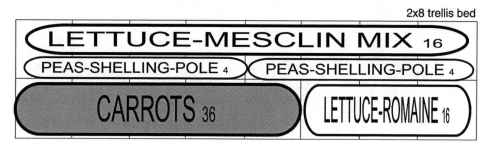

3x8 raised bed

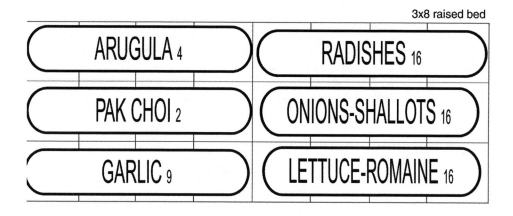

3x8 raised bed

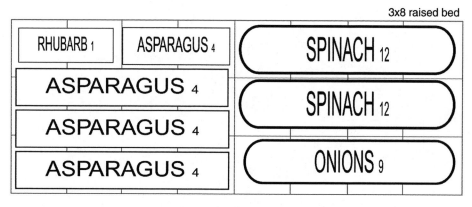

Instant Organic Garden - Plant-a-Gram™

Chapter 12
Building Your Garden Beds

Once you know how many raised and trellis beds you'll need you're ready to get started. A variety of materials can be used, and each has pros and cons. Untreated wood is cheap but attracts termites and will rot after only a few years. Cedar and redwood won't rot, but they're expensive and hard to find in most areas. Bricks, cinder blocks, and stone are other materials to consider, but they are expensive, too, and can have sharp edges.

In my opinion, your most affordable option is pressure-treated decking. Although on its own, the decking is not ideal for organic gardening, you can use some black plastic to line the inner walls so the chemicals used to pressure-treat the wood won't leach into your garden. It's affordable, easy to find, and easy to work with. *Just make sure you don't breathe the sawdust, burn it or put it in your compost pile.*

WARNING!

Railroad ties, which are treated the poison creosote, should not be used in vegetable gardens; if you know someone who's using them, tell him or her to convert the beds to grow flowers or shrubs and start over elsewhere in the yard.

Bed Construction

Choose your final garden site in an area in your yard with at least six hours of sun and as close to your back door and a water source as possible. The beds should face south and the trellis and tall plants should be on the north side so they won't cast shadows on the other plants during the day. *NOTE: Mowing the grass on your garden site will make things easier.*

Materials list

Four 12-foot pieces of 5½-by-1½-inch pressure-treated decking, each cut into a three-foot and a nine-foot section.

One eight-foot pressure-treated 2x4, cut into six 16-inch pieces.

One very small roll of black plastic.

30 1¾-inch decking screws.

Instructions

Assemble the two long sides of your beds first by laying the 2x4s on the ground and attaching the rails with your decking screws as shown. Then set them up on a level surface and attach the two sets of shorter side rails.

Front View...

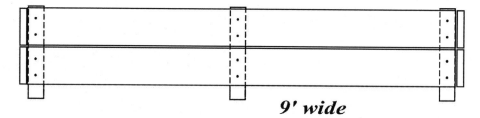

9' wide

Top View...

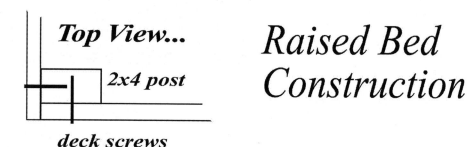

2x4 post

deck screws

Raised Bed Construction

Bring the finished bed to your garden site and make note of where the posts and rails hit the ground. A trick is to sprinkle lime around the inside bottom of the bed to mark the ground.

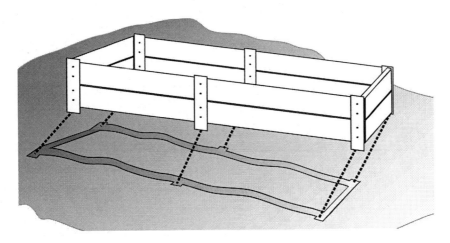

Set your bed aside and create space for your rails in your sod by digging a two-inch-wide trench that starts an inch below the lowest spot in the bed. Continue around the perimeter, keeping the trench level. In each inside corner, dig a deeper hole to accept the lower part of each 2x4 post. You'll also need holes for your posts in the inside middle of each side. *NOTE: Don't remove your grass since that will expose weeds to sunlight and allow them to germinate. The only exception would be bermuda grass or an area with lots of weeds. In that case, scrape down to bare soil.*

With the trench and holes dug, insert the bed and check for level. You'll never get it right the first time! Keep digging and leveling until you have it right. Then staple a layer of plastic sheeting to the interior side of each rail. Don't put plastic on the bottom of your bed; that makes a pond, not a garden.

Trellis Beds

In order to make your raised bed garden a trellis bed, all you need to do is switch the back two corners for 8' tall posts. You can use 2x4 or 4x4 lumber. You'll need to attach a 2x4 crosspiece across the top to hold your trellis netting. Netting is available online.

I recommend netting that looks like fishing line. It resists UV rays so it lasts a while. The openings are 6" square, so it's easy to put your hand through when harvesting. Weave the netting through your 2x4 crosspiece before you attach it.

Building the beds is the hardest part of getting a garden started. From now on, all you have to do is plant seeds and water as needed.

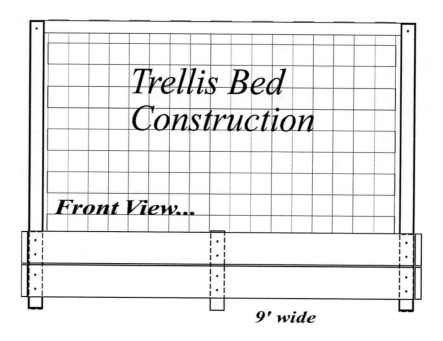

Trellis Bed Construction

Front View...

9' wide

Soil Components

Choosing the right soil is the most important part of a successful garden, and because you're using raised beds you can control the mix completely.

You have two options...

1. Potting mix.

Most mixes contain compost, peat moss, pine bark and perlite in varying amounts. They're all pretty good, but don't be fooled into paying a premium for "organic" potting mix. Almost any mix you buy will be organic. You want to avoid any with synthetic fertilizers. They'll say "plant food added" or "slow release fertilizer included," or "feeds your plants for three months." These will cause the unnatural plant growth problems discussed in previous chapters. And some of these slow release fertilizers are heat activated and will burn new plants during the heat of summer.

2. Compost and sand.

I don't like potting mixes that contain peat moss, since it has a property that makes it hard to get wet, and there are concerns about how it is harvested. Another option is a 75% / 25% mixture of compost and sand. Quality compost can be found in bulk in many areas and is a lot less expensive than bags of potting mix. Many cities now collect yard waste and compost it to produce an excellent product.

They test their compost regularly and because they are able to get their piles to decompose completely under high temperatures weed seeds and pathogens are eliminated.

If you have to buy your compost in bags, instead of getting 12 of the same material, consider getting a mix of different types. Whether it's cow manure, chicken litter, or mushroom compost, each kind has it's own chemical profile and blending several together gives you a much more balanced product. Just avoid anything with "biosolids" as an ingredient. It's sewage sludge!

Sand can also be purchased in bulk and, if you have a choice, "river sand" is your best bet. If you have to resort to using bags, play sand is OK, but we probably don't want to be using cement sand.

No "Topsoil"
Topsoil is *not* a good choice because you have no idea what it really is. It can be composted bio-waste, or topsoil from your area that contains thousands of dormant weed seeds.

Topsoil is not a good choice because you have no idea what it really is!

Organic Fertilizers
You'll want to add slow release organic fertilizers to your soil. Worm castings are an excellent choice, but balanced organic fertilizers that contain micro-nutrients such as Plant-Tone are good choices, too.

Filling the Bed
First, water the grass inside the bed and cover it with three layers of non-glossy newspaper. Wet the newspaper to keep it in place and start adding the soil mix. If your mix includes peat moss, add water as you go and use a rake to get it well distributed. When you get to the top four inches, start blending in your fertilizer.

As discussed above, peat moss is hard to get wet and needs a little help at first. For compost and sand mixtures you can wait and water your new bed once it's full. Continue until the soil is within an inch of the top of the rails.

You can also activate your soil with a "drench" of liquid fertilizer. Fish emulsion and seaweed blends are commonly available. Your kids can get involved in almost all aspects of building and filling your beds. They love to add the water!

How nature works - layers of soil

Head out to a nearby wooded area and bring a shovel. Show how leaves act as a mulch, and as they rot, become compost, and how this all makes the soil below dark and rich. Dig even deeper to find the less fertile subsoil. Explain how you use the same layers of compost, mulch, rich soil and subsoil in your own garden. Add more organic fertilizer at the end of each season and some more compost as mulch in the summer and you'll never have to till again!

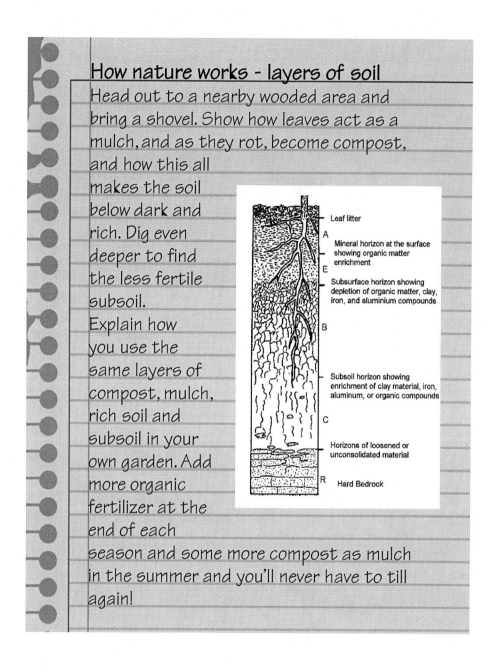

Leaf litter

A
Mineral horizon at the surface showing organic matter enrichment
E
Subsurface horizon showing depletion of organic matter, clay, iron, and aluminium compounds

B

Subsoil horizon showing enrichment of clay material, iron, aluminum, or organic compounds

C

Horizons of loosened or unconsolidated material

R   Hard Bedrock

Chapter 13
Planting and Plant Care

When to Plant

Knowing when to plant is one of the most important keys to successful gardening. Plant too soon and your seeds will rot in cold, damp soil. If you wait too late, your cool season crops may take too long to mature and burn up in the summer heat.

You can look at the map in Chapter 9 to determine the last winter frost dates for your general area. Of course this will vary from year to year, but you can get a good idea of what to expect. You plant your summer crop seeds a few days after your last frost date and when you set in tomato, pepper and eggplant transplants be prepared to cover them if an unexpected frost seems imminent.

If your last frost date is April 15th, you want to time your spring crops to be finishing up by then. Since most cool season crops need two months to begin their harvest that means you should plant your spring crops two months prior to your first frost, in this case February 15th.

Your summer plants will continue to produce until the first fall frost kills them, so look at the map to get an idea of when that will occur. Your fall crops will grow through freezing weather, but you want to get them well established before the coldest temperatures set in. (*See Seasonal Transitions in Chapter 14, to learn tricks on how to plant seeds for fall while still harvesting summer crops.*)

If your first fall frost date is November 1st, you'll want to plant your fall seeds about two and a half months earlier, around August 15th. Winter crops can be planted in areas where temperatures don't get too extreme – usually a month after your fall planting, although some winter crops like brussels sprouts are planted at fall planting time.

Planting Seeds

I advocate starting all garden crops from seed except for the big three – tomatoes, peppers and eggplants. This is where your children get involved. Depending on their ages and skill levels, they can help you in almost every stage of the process.

Your first step is to set aside a small bucket of soil mix and then smooth out the rest of your new garden so the soil is about an inch from the top of the rails. I use a slat from a peach crate to smooth out the soil.

Transfer your garden layout to your soil by drawing lines for the border of each planting area. The peach crate slat is great for drawing straight lines in soil, too.

Start with the back of the bed and sprinkle any tiny seeds (*carrots, lettuce, etc.*) evenly over the area marked out for each crop.

Larger seeds can be placed evenly in rows for climbing plants, or in the middle of the section for larger plants like squash. When you're happy with their placement, just "push and pinch" – push each seed about ½" below the surface and pinch the soil over top to cover each seed completely.

Garlic or shallot bulbs and onion sets are placed root side down. Space them evenly and press them into the soil until their tops are below the surface.

When your bed is seeded, take the soil you set aside and cover all your areas with tiny seeds with 1/8" to 1/4" of soil. Pat it all down to ensure good seed to soil contact and then give everything a good drink of water.

Planting Thick and Thin

Our goal is to find ways to get a lot of productivity out of a small garden. Ideally, we want a lot of harvest over a long period of time. A great way to do this, especially with a spring garden, is to plant "thick and thin" - plant thickly and then eat the thinnings as an early harvest.

Lettuce is a good example...

If you plan for one plant every ten to twelve inches like the seed package says, you'll end up with a one day harvest. You'll plant your seeds, wait seven weeks, harvest your lettuce and have a bare spot in your garden until it's time to plant your summer crops.

Instead of planting one seed, plant 25 per square foot. In a few weeks they'll have sprouted and you'll have a nice carpet of baby plants. As they grow to about three inches tall they'll start to crowd each other a bit. That's when you get out your scissors and start to thin. Clip every other plant above the root and put it in your harvest basket. *(If you pull them out by the roots you'll disturb the*

plants
nearby
and you'll
also get
dirt in your
lettuce!)

This is not a precise process. If one area is planted more thickly than another, that's where you do the most thinning. If you've planted different varieties of lettuce and you have five or six square feet planted, you'll have enough organic baby lettuce leaves for an excellent salad every night of the week!

Wait a few more days until the remaining 12 plants per foot have grown up a bit more - perhaps to four inches. Again, take out your scissors and snip out every other one. There will be fewer plants, but they'll be larger, so you'll have another nice harvest.

Now you have six plants left. Let each of these continue to develop and pull an entire plant every evening until there's only one or two left in the middle of your square.

That's when you start your "North, South, East, West" method. Don't harvest the entire plant, just take a leaf from the north side of each plant on one day, another leaf from the south side the next day, and so on throughout the rest of the cool weather growing season.

This works with more than just lettuce. You can do the same trick with spinach, onions (*harvest the young plants as scallions*) and carrots. By planting thick and eating your thinnings you'll have an early harvest that will continue all season long!

Watering your garden

Another regularly asked question is "*How often should I water my garden?*" Watering is not something you should do at a set time interval or with a sprinkler system.

Instead, you need to learn how to tell when a plant is thirsty or your soil is dry. A thirsty plant's leaves will be dull and droop just a little. You can also stick a finger into your soil to test the moisture. Watering every day will cause your plants to have shallow roots and if it gets hot or you can't water for a few days they'll be in big trouble.

Wait until your plants are a little bit thirsty and give them a good soaking with a water wand. This will encourage them to send roots deep into the soil where they will pick up more nutrients and resist dry spells.

This approach of "water seldom, water deeply" applies to lawns and shrubs as well. Encouraging deep root growth is one of the best things you can do for any outdoor plant.

Watering Frequency

Perform an experiment with watering and root growth. Take two seeds and plant them in identical pots. Water one plant with 1/3 cup every day and the other with one cup every three days. Compare the results in growth and productivity. At the end of the season pull out the plants and examine how the roots grew.

Chapter 14
Gardening Through the Year

Now that you've built your raised bed garden and planted your first seeds, what will you need to do on an ongoing basis? The good news is when you start with perfect soil there's no need for digging and tilling each season.

Maintaining Soil Fertility

So how do you keep your garden growing strong? A clue can be found by watching Nature. As we discussed, the forest has layers of leaves, composted leaves, black topsoil and red clay subsoil that form naturally. The worms and bacteria break down the leaves and add all the fertility that's needed.

The good news is when you start with perfect soil there's no need for digging and tilling each season...

This model can be applied to your back yard garden. Each season I recommend the use of organic, slow-release fertilizer with micronutrients included. (*Plant-Tone is a good brand*). Scratch a couple of cups into the top inch or two of soil. In the summer, add a one to two inch layer of compost as mulch. This has the benefit of adding more organic matter to the soil; it adds fertility and also helps keep weeds down and conserves moisture. Just like in the forest, your garden will have layers of compost, black topsoil, and native soil below. The worms and other life in the soil will take the nutrients throughout your garden and every year the soil will get richer and richer.

So what kind of compost is best? There are lots to choose from - mushroom compost, cow manure, pine-bark compost and poultry litter, to name a few. You don't need a lot, three inexpensive bags of compost will cover 60 square feet of garden space 1½ inches deep. I suggest you try the trick of making "super compost."

Each kind of compost has its own chemical profile with different strengths and weaknesses. Instead of buying three bags of one type, buy one each of three kinds of compost at a local garden center. Any variety will do and they're generally not very expensive. Mix them together for a better-balanced product.

Resist the urge to pull out the tiller every season to pulverize your soil and bring weed seeds to the surface. Instead, add some organic fertilizer and, in the summer, a layer of blended compost. You'll add fertility to the soil and cut down on weeding, while conserving moisture.

Seasonal Transitions

Moving from one season to another is like a complicated dance. You want to continue to harvest your mature crops, but if you wait until they're all finished it will be too late to start seeds for the next season.

Summer to Fall

Believe it or not, the heat of the summer is the right time to start planting your *fall* garden. Many people think of vegetable gardening as a spring and summer activity, but throughout most of the United States you can have successful crops all four seasons.

Many people think of vegetable gardening as a spring and summer project, but throughout most of the United States you can have successful crops all four seasons.

The fall garden is one of the most rewarding. By the time the plants are productive most of the bugs will be gone and harvesting is done in much cooler weather. What can you grow in the fall? Think salads and you're off to a good start. Imagine a lettuce salad with arugula, carrots, radishes and even some spinach thrown in, all organic, and all right from your own back yard.

If you already have a garden, you don't want to pull up your summer crops. You'll still be picking tomatoes, peppers and eggplants until the first frost. Just before you plant your fall seeds, clear out everything you can. Remove the lower ranches of tomato plants, pull out that last squash plant (*admit it, you're sick of squash anyway!*) and clean up your soil. This is a great time to sprinkle on some slow release, organic fertilizer and mix it into the top inch or two of your soil.

As described before, set aside some fine soil and smooth out your bed. Mark where the new crops will go and sprinkle them in place, covering them with your extra soil. Pat it down for good contact. Fall seeds won't like the high temperatures of summer, but your summer plants will cool the soil by offering a bit of shade.

Here's the most important part - *water lightly twice a day for the next two weeks.* I know I said earlier that you should water deeply and less often, but with severe summer heat sometimes the tiny seeds will have trouble germinating, and if they do, the little seedlings can dry up before they put down good roots. In springtime this isn't as important since the soil is cool and moist at night and the morning dew waters your seedlings automatically.

So use a light misting spray and give a good drink of water to all your tiny seeds while they're germinating and getting started. Once everything is up and growing you can move back to deep watering every few days as needed.

Finally, keep an eye on things. If the high temperatures continue, consider adding some shade to your garden in the afternoon. Anything you have around will do - an old screen, an old door, a tarp. The idea is not to cover the garden, but to stand something up to the side to shelter the garden from the afternoon sun. Any light past 3pm on a hot day is not going to be much help to your fall seeds and seedlings.

Fall to Winter

In most parts of the country you can have a winter garden as well. If you have any summer plants that are remaining, you should remove them now and clean up any leaves or dropped fruit. *NOTE: Diseased or insect infested plants or leaves should be thrown into the trash and not a compost pile or left in your garden.*

Your winter garden plan will be similar to your fall crops, so it may be as simple as planting those seeds again in the bare spots you've created. This is also the time to plant garlic, onions and shallot bulbs as well as your berries – blueberries, blackberries, raspberries and strawberries. Plants can be purchased locally as established transplants or by mail as bare root plants. Check with local nurseries for information about your area. *See the Appendix for more information on specific plants.*

Winter to Spring

With traditional gardens, you have to wait until the soil is warm and until it is "dry enough to be worked." Tilling or working in moist, spring soil will cause clumps to form, which makes your work almost impossible. Because you have raised beds your soil will warm two weeks earlier and since your soil is already excellent, there's no need for tilling or digging.

As with the fall to winter transition, clear out plants that have finished producing, add slow release organic fertilizer and sprinkle in your seeds. Cover with your mix and make sure the seeds stay moist as they germinate.

Spring to Summer

Start your summer garden when the danger of frost is over. Again, you will still have spring crops producing a bountiful harvest at this time and you don't want to pull everything up to make room for the next season.

The answer is to harvest smart. Take note of where your tomatoes, peppers, eggplants and squash will be in your summer garden and harvest the spring crops from those spots. Pop in your transplants and as they grow, continue to remove spring plants in concentric circles. As the summer warms up, your new plants may be able to provide a bit of shade for your spring crops and extend your spring harvest!

If you have a row of spring peas and you have string beans or cucumbers planned for summer, just plant the new seeds on the other side of your trellis. By the time the string beans and cucumbers are starting to climb, your peas should be done. Just remove the vines carefully.

If your summer garden is in full afternoon sun and your veggies tend to burn up, consider a living shade curtain. Plant some sunflowers in a spot outside your garden where they'll cast afternoon shade as they grow. If you find they're providing too much shade, you can always remove one or several plants.

Don.

> ## Planting Sunflowers?
> Make a sunflower fort for your kids. Instead of a straight row of plants, arrange them in a box or circle about four feet across. As the plants grow they'll make a great fort or hiding place for younger children!

Dealing with the heat

Every summer it seems like there's a heat wave that threatens to roast your entire garden. What to do?

1 *Don't Over Water.* Resist the temptation to drown your plants to keep them from drying out. It's normal for leaves to droop in the heat of the day. Instead use a water wand to apply water deeply every few days. You *should* be concerned if your plants are drooping in the morning.

2 *Mulch, Mulch, Mulch!* Mulching keeps the moisture in and the heat down. A light colored mulch is better than a dark one. I recommend using a blend of compost materials.

3 *Don't Fertilize!* Fertilizing, especially when you use non-organic mixes, will cause your plants to add new growth, even if they don't want to. Summer heat can cause "slow-release" synthetic fertilizers to release rapidly and burn your plants' roots.

4 *Be Patient.* Your tomatoes may stop producing. This is temporary and they'll resume their work once the temperatures move back down. Tomatoes need evening temperatures below 70° in order to set fruit.

5 *Personal Safety.* Use common sense and stay out of the garden during the heat of the day. If you do have to go out, wear a big floppy hat and light colored clothes and drink lots of water.

6 *Water Restrictions?* Set up a water barrel to collect rainwater. Use it for your thirstiest plants first. Rainwater is *much* better than city water because it doesn't have chlorine or other chemicals.

7 *Plan for Next Year.* If summer heat seems to be a consistent problem, you should consider relocating your garden to a spot that gets at least six hours of sun, but where it also gets afternoon shade. Mix lots of compost into your soil to allow for better water retention and deeper root growth. Choose heat resistant plants and place them closer together so they'll shade each other. Water deeply and less often to encourage deep root growth.

Chapter 15
Other Gardening Issues

Composting, Yes or No?

Should you start a compost pile? Here are some quick thoughts on the subject...

Compost is black gold. Gardeners add it to their existing soil to turn it into rich, garden loam. However, since I advocate raised beds and new potting mix to start a garden, the old method of tilling up your poor soil and incorporating a lot of compost is no longer needed. The native soil often contains thousands of viable weed seeds so adding compost and fertilizer just makes them grow that much faster. You end up with a weed patch instead of a garden!

Instead I use compost during the summer as mulch only. I spread out a top layer of about two inches and leave it alone. The nutrients break down over time to feed the soil naturally, and the mulch serves to keep the soil moist. Let your worms eat the compost and do the tilling for you! So the amount of compost I need for my garden is not very great.

Let your worms eat the compost and do the tilling for you!

Don't get me wrong, composting is a lot of fun. It's very emotionally satisfying to take kitchen scraps and yard waste and turn it into gardening gold. The question is whether it's right for your family and the situation in your garden. Do you have the time to take on an additional project? If so, read on.

To get you started, I need to explain that there are two kinds of compost piles - hot and cold. *Hot composting* is a pile that really starts cooking. The heat comes from the microbial action as the various materials decompose. The good news is that this heat (*over 140°*) kills off weed seeds and harmful bacteria and you will have usable material in three to eight weeks. The bad news is that the pile will need to be turned regularly in order to heat up. Also, the heat will kill some of the good bacteria along with the bad. If you don't turn it often your pile won't reach the proper temperature and there will be material at the edges that never gets cooked. You'll need a pile measuring at least three feet in each direction to move things along at a good pace. With a small yard you may never accumulate the amount of material you need for a good pile. So hot composting may not be worth the work.

Cold composting is a lot easier to do, but it takes much more time - often up to a full year. You simply make a pile and keep adding to it whenever you have the material. It's less work and you don't end up killing as many good bacteria, but the big problem is that many of the weed seeds survive quite nicely. If you use grass clippings as a compost ingredient, realize that every weed seed landing in your yard gets sucked into your mower. If you have a weed-free garden and you add cold compost to it you might as well be planting weeds! But if you don't put any material in your pile that has weeds, cold composting is a good way to go.

Another alternative is to use one of those composting systems in a box, tub or tumbler. They can produce good compost in two to three weeks using a small amount of material, and turning it is simple - you just roll the box or turn a handle. But the cost of these systems, sometimes over $200, makes me think twice.

If you decide to start a compost pile anyway, that's great! It's a lot of fun and educational for your kids. You need three things, compostible material, air and moisture. For the materials you need to think of lasagna. First add a thin layer of green, then a thick layer of brown and put some soil or finished compost on top. Green provides the nitrogen. (*Grass clippings or vegetable scraps are good sources.*) Brown is the carbon. (*Dry leaves or sawdust are examples.*) The soil or finished compost is used to inoculate the pile with bacteria and good bugs. When you add something like kitchen scraps, make sure you cover it with leaves or other material to allow the composting process to begin.

A key to successful composting is to make sure there is plenty of air and moisture. A proper pile should never smell bad. That means it's not getting enough air. You can fix this by initially placing your pile on something that raises it off the ground a bit, an old pallet, or larger twigs in a pile. Some people put perforated tubes throughout their piles to let in air. Others take a special composting tool and shove it and back out again to create an airway.

If the pile is getting enough air, but it doesn't seem to be doing much, it may be because it's not getting enough moisture. The pile should be kept moist just like garden soil - not too wet, though.

Compost piles are very health conscious vegetarians - no meat, no fat, and no thick branches. Make sure the individual pieces are small sized. Many people will mow over a pile of leaves and shred them before putting them into the pile. Another trick is to store dried leaves in plastic bags and crush before adding them. And no chemicals - if you ever have pressure treated wood don't add the sawdust and if you've just had your lawn chemically treated (*shame on you!*), discard those grass clippings. Finally, vegetarian animal manures are fine (*rabbits*), but nothing from dogs or cats, they contain harmful pathogens.

The big difference between a hot pile and a cold one is how often it's turned. Both need to be at least a cubic yard in size – and larger is better. Many people use a three bin system. They make a cage of some sort and throw in their initial layers, wait a couple of weeks and then turn everything over into the second bin. New material can go into the first bin. They repeat the process 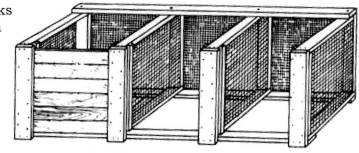 into the third bin a couple of weeks later. After two more weeks they sift the finished compost through a ½" wire mesh. Anything that remains behind is put back into the first bin for another full round. Rocks and glass are discarded and clumps are broken up.

One trick is to store fall leaves in bags in a dry place over the winter and start your pile in the spring. You take the grass clippings and your leaves and some soil (*compost is much better for this*) and you're off and running.

If you end up making cold compost just remember that if you use grass clippings it will be full of weed seeds. Plan to

use it somewhere where the weeds won't bother you.
Using the tumbler is pretty much the same as hot
composting, just with smaller amounts of material
and faster results. The same mix of materials is used
and the same prohibitions are observed.

Let it Rot!

If you add kitchen scraps, take
something recognizable, like an apple
core or banana peel and place it in a
specific spot in your compost pile.
Cover with a layer of shredded leaves.
Return every day or so and pull back
the leaves. Make note of how rapidly
the material decomposes.

Pests in the Garden

So you've built your raised bed garden, filled it with perfect
soil and your seeds have sprouted into lush green plants.
It turns out you're not the only one eyeing your fresh, tasty
vegetables – there are all sorts of critters out there hoping
to make a meal out of your entire garden. There's nothing
more frustrating than walking out to your lettuce patch,
only to find little stubs!

Who's after your veggies, and what are safest ways to
protect the harvest?

It helps to put the culprits into several groups – bugs,
critters and pets. Bugs are a real pain, but they don't eat
your entire garden overnight, and there are organic pesticides and other controls you can learn to use effectively.
It's best to focus on the bigger critters – usually furry ones,
who can eat up your entire garden overnight.

Deer and rabbits are by far the most destructive pests in
the home garden. If it weren't for that movie Bambi, and
the fact that they're called deer instead of "yard rats,"
people might see deer as the pests they are, instead of
something cute and cuddly that need to be protected.
According to the National Highway Traffic Safety
Administration there are about 1.5 million car accidents

with deer each year that result in $1 billion in vehicle damage, about 150 human fatalities, and over 10,000 personal injuries.

So how do you know if your damage is from deer or rabbits? Examine the leaves. Deer crush their food, so the remains would be torn and shredded. Rabbits have sharp little teeth and their damage looks like scissors have sliced each stem.

Another way to tell is to look for droppings. Rabbits leave little pea sized pellets, while deer leave oval shapes that are less than an inch long.

Deterring Deer

The goal is to discourage feeding from the start. You don't want them to think of your yard as a buffet. Drastic remedies include 6' -10' high fencing and electronic devices which can be very effective in severe cases. There are lots of home remedies including hair and soap.

A good one to try is very simple. Take an egg white and mix it well into a gallon of water and spray that around your yard. It will smell like rotten eggs, but is so diluted only the deer will notice. Dogs are also good deer deterrents.

There are all sorts of products you can buy to protect your garden from deer. The stranger ones I've seen are coyote and mountain lion urine – doesn't appeal to me much! Most are not organic and shouldn't be used on garden crops.

Rabbits

Rabbits cause lots of garden damage. You leave your lettuce and spinach in the evening and in the morning all that's left are little green stumps – very frustrating! The good news is that rabbits are easier to repel than deer. In fact, the most common ingredient in commercial repellants is something you can

buy at the
garden center. Blood meal is just that – dried blood.
Sounds awful, but the smell drives rabbits away and it's
also an organic fertilizer. Even better is the fact that it
costs a lot less than commercial repellants – a five pound
bag might be $5, vs. $15. The only problem is that you
may have to reapply after a rain, but it's fertilizer, so it
does some good for your garden.

Squirrels

Squirrels are often seen digging in the garden, but they're
usually burying or digging up nuts, not hurting your
plants – at least not on purpose. Many
of my clients report squirrels will eat
their tomatoes, especially in a
drought. They're usually just thirsty
and are after tomatoes for their water
content. A simple solution is to put out a
pan of water. They'll drink it instead of
ruining your tomatoes!

Organic Critter Controls

There have been significant advances in organic controls
for deer, rabbits, squirrels and even dogs and cats. One
company I heartily recommend is **www.imustgarden.com,**
which has a full line of safe sprays you can use directly on
edible plants.

Gardening for the Handicapped

Someone asked me the other day, "*Do you have any garden
bed designs for the handicapped?*" I thought about it for a
while and I decided that I had to adjust my thinking. I was
visualizing a raised bed garden on some sort of platform or
table that would be easily accessible. I then realized that
once the plants started to grow, especially on a trellis bed,
the work would quickly be out of reach.

I looked at a trellis bed and asked myself about what is
actually required for this new style of organic garden. Once
the bed is built, there's no digging or tilling. Since the soil
is weedless, there's no weeding. The only work required is
planting seeds, which requires a bit of bending down, and
watering, which can be done from any height using a water
wand. There's very little tending of the plants short of some
pruning of tomatoes and such until harvest time, which

is done at chest or eye level. My answer is that because there is so little work involved with weedless raised or trellis beds, almost anyone, even with some handicaps, can be a successful gardener.

Restaurant Gardens, Church Gardens, and Community Gardens

My approach to making gardening easy can apply to more than just families. Restaurants are noting a steadily increasing interest in organic produce from their clientele. But the few organic farms in the area find it hard to keep up with commercial demand. Restaurant owners would like to start their own gardens, but the workload is just too much when using the traditional approach. Gardens using raised beds and weedless soil can reduce the workload to planting once a season, and then watering as needed. Harvesting can be done daily as needed, so everything will always be fresh. And believe me, the customers will notice the difference in flavor.

My approach to making gardening easy can apply to more than just families.

They could start with basic crops like lettuce mixes and spinach, along with a variety of herbs like rosemary and basil, and add more crops and beds as needed. The garden will be so neat and tidy they could invite their clients to take a tour while they wait for their tables. Their organic garden could be promoted in their menu - "today's organic salad greens were harvested from our own garden." Organic gardening is of such interest that it's likely to attract local publicity.

I've talked with several churches interested in starting gardens to feed the homeless. Because there is so little work, the gardens are easy to maintain and are very productive in a small amount of space. They can even set aside a part of their garden for congregants to use as a community garden. And what pastor or minister wouldn't like more visitors to his church each week?

Community gardens can also benefit from this approach. Often gardens using native soil are kept up for the first month or two, but once the weather gets hot the number of visits decrease and the weeds start to grow out of control. Members find it hard to get to their gardens four or five times a week to do all the weeding. **Raised beds, weedless soil** means these gardens can be managed with much less work, making everyone a lot happier.

Appendix
Plant Care and Tips

Most plants are easy to grow. Make sure you have the right soil and light conditions, plant the seeds the right distance apart and you're good to go. But some crops need a bit of extra attention – either with planting, crop maintenance, harvesting, or all three. Here are some you might need to know more about...

Asparagus

Growing and harvesting asparagus is a balancing act. You want to enjoy a good harvest, but you also need to make sure you don't deplete the strength of the plants.

Start with two year old crowns, male plants are most productive. Plant them five inches apart and six inches deep. Spread the thick roots out carefully and cover with soil. The first year they'll send up skinny little shoots, which aren't very good for eating. Let them grow up into ferns which will soak up the sun all spring and summer and send energy into the roots.

By September your asparagus should be bright green ferns three to five feet tall. You may see some red berries as well. Once the weather starts to cool down your ferns will start to turn a bit brown and die back. Cut them off at the bottom and throw the ferns away. If you let the berries drop to the ground, you'll have tiny little asparagus plants starting in your garden next year, so feel free to dispose of the ferns in the trash unless you have a hot compost pile.

After their first year, they'll use their stored energy to send up thicker spears - starting with pencil thickness. These are great to eat - tender and tasty! Use a sharp knife to cut them off below the surface before the buds start to open out into the beginnings of branches. Every time you cut a spear, another will pop up to take its place. If you harvest too long you'll deplete the plant's energy, so go easy the first year. Enjoy those thin shoots for 3 - 6 weeks.

The next year is when you'll be getting a significant harvest of pinky or finger sized shoots. Perfect! Here's the other side of the balancing act. If you *stop* harvesting too soon, the plants will send up big ferns and put a lot of energy into the roots. The next year the spears would be thick as a thumb and after that - a big toe!

Once your asparagus are established, your goal is to keep continuing your harvest for a long time so the plants don't get too big. That's why I plant them so close together originally. We want them to crowd together and compete for nutrients and not become gigantic. What a wonderful problem to have - a long harvest period for your tender, tasty asparagus!

Blueberries

Blueberries are the perfect food. Besides their fantastic taste, by now almost everyone has heard about the health benefits of blueberries – plenty of vitamins, high in antioxidants, to name a few. But did you know that blueberries are one of the easiest plants to manage? They have beautiful foliage – especially in the fall. They're simple to grow, they rarely suffer from bugs or diseases and they'll produce for years and years with only minimal maintenance.

There are two main types of blueberries, rabbiteye and highbush. Rabbiteyes are better in warmer climates and highbush do better in the north, in mountains and along the coast. Check with your garden center for what's best in your area. Whichever you choose, plant several cultivars. Different plants will cross-pollinate producing a greater harvest.

Here's a trick. Choose plants in groups of three and select early, middle, and late maturing varieties. Your garden center should be able to tell you which is which. Instead of harvesting twenty pounds of berries over two weeks and running the risk of having too much of a good thing, you can end up with a similar harvest over a four or even five week period. Look for one gallon plants at your local hardware store or garden center. A fair price is $10 - $15.

Planting blueberries is easy, but takes a few steps to get the best results. Blueberries like full to partial sun, acid,

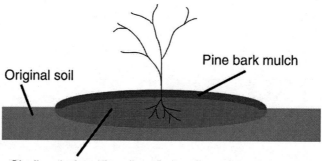

Original soil

Pine bark mulch

Shallow hole with soil and pine fine mix

well-drained soil and they don't like weeds. Here's how to proceed.

1 Remove and discard your sod and dig a shallow hole six inches at the deepest point. Set the dirt aside.

2 Poke some holes in the ground to improve drainage. Get a matching amount of ground pine bark – often called "soil conditioner." It's the fine material left over from processing pine bark nuggets and often comes in two cubic foot bags. Also pick up some Holly-Tone or other organic fertilizer that is for acid-loving plants like azaleas. Mix it all together and place it in your hole. You should end up with a mound of soil.

3 Remove your blueberry plant from its pot. Tease the roots a bit if they're crowded, and plant it so it is at the same level it was in the pot, which means it will be some-what above the original soil level. Mulch with two inches of pine bark nuggets, but don't bury the stem.

4 Make sure you keep them well watered as they become established. Place the plants about five feet apart.

As they grow, remove any crossing branches, and any three year old canes (*they'll be woody looking and have deteriorating bark*). Then sit back and wait for a fantastic harvest of blueberries every summer for years to come!

Carrots

Carrots are lots of fun to grow and are very popular with the kids. Here are some tips that will help...

1 *Planting Depth.* Carrots are tiny seeds and need to be planted at a shallow depth. Take a cup of existing soil from your bed, smooth out what remains and carefully cast your seeds evenly across your target area. Sprinkle your soil lightly over your seeds and press it all in gently.

2 *Watering.* Carrots are like grass seed. They need to stay moist during the germination period, which means you should mist them lightly once or twice a day for the first week to ten days. If a seed starts to sprout and dries out - even for a day - it will be dead and gone.

3 *Rabbits.* If you see evidence of rabbits eating your carrots you can sprinkle blood meal around your carrot patch. Rabbits hate the smell and the blood meal is a fertilizer. You'll need to reapply it after it rains.

4 *Thinning.* Once your carrots are about six inches high, you may find that some that are a bit too close together. You should pull up a few and see if they're big enough to eat as baby carrots. If so, you can thin your carrot patch to where the carrots are about two inches apart.

5 *Harvesting.* As your carrots tops reach about a foot tall they'll start to be ready to harvest. Again, you can pull a few and see how big they are, or you can just slide your finger down the stem and feel for the orange shoulder of the carrot. That will give you a good idea of how big the carrot has become.

6 *Planting times.* Carrots take about two seasons to mature, and they can be planted almost any time. Plan your garden to have somewhat of a permanent carrot patch, so if you start to thin them out, you can drop in some more seeds. Just remember to keep them watered for their first 7-10 days!

Herbs

Herbs are very popular for the home garden. Since most of them have Mediterranean origins they need lean, well-drained soil instead of the super-fertile soil in our raised beds. An herb's job is to produce leaves, which is a lot easier than generating fruits like tomatoes, squash or peppers. Also, many herbs grow over more than a single season. Our beds are designed for production vegetables, which are planted and grown over a single season only to be removed and replaced by the next season's crops. I advocate growing your herbs in pots or separate planters. Use a leaner soil mix – 50% compost and 50% sand is an option as well as 50% potting mix and 50% sand. Don't add any fertilizers or potting mix that has fertilizers included.

All About Herbs

Herbs are especially popular with the kids. The fact that a green plant can smell like a yellow lemon is amazing to them. The variety of scents and flavors is incredible. When considering an herb garden, first show them the herbs you use with your own family cooking, like basil and oregano for spaghetti sauce and pizza, or mint for iced tea. Then take them on a field trip to a good garden center that sells a wide selection of herbs. Teach them how to rub the leaves and smell the scents of different herbs. Pick out the herbs you need for your garden, but let them choose some varieties for themselves. They'll have a ball inviting their friends to rub the leaves to guess what the flavors are!

Avoid clay pots. They dry out *very* quickly. You may end up having to water twice a day and your plants will go from very dry to very wet in a short time. Instead go with plastic pots - many look just like clay, and they're lighter and inexpensive.

Use water crystals. They absorb water and release it slowly as needed. They're available at garden centers under different names like *Terra-Sorb* and *Soil Moist*. Add the crystals to your soil as indicated on the package.

Instead of buying a whole packet of seeds to grow just a few plants, I suggest you head out to the garden center in the spring and look through the variety of herbs to choose from as transplants. Rub a leaf or two and get a sense of how each smells and tastes. Get three types of basil and give them all a try. Remember that most herbs are happiest when they're used on a regular basis, so pinch often and don't let them get away from you.

Squash

Squash is usually easy to grow. Plant three seeds close together, thin down to the strongest plant and you're in business. But right at the point where you're getting a great harvest, suddenly the plant drops dead with no warning at all!

The cause is squash vine borers, one of the most annoying pests in the garden. I haven't found any good ways to kill them that won't hurt your bees. Usually they do their damage late in the season when you're sick of squash anyway.

If you want to try to overcome these pests, here are some suggestions. Squash vine borers are moths that lay masses of tiny orange eggs underneath the leaves of your squash plants. The eggs hatch and little larvae crawl down and bore into the stem. They munch away and eat out the stem from the inside. As long as some stem remains the plant will continue to grow. Once it's severed, the plant drops dead "all at once."

1 Look for the orange eggs under the leaves. Remove the leaf section and/or smash the eggs.

2 When the plants first start out bury the stems in more soil. This will keep the bugs away and also encourage rooting so if one part of the stem is severed, the plant will still get water.

3 Some people have tried to wrap the stems in aluminum foil, or laying aluminum foil under the plant to confuse the moths. I even saw something online about covering the stem with shaving cream to prevent entry!

4 If the larvae get inside you'll see orange sawdust material around the stem. You can perform surgery on the plant by slicing into the stem lengthwise (*not across!*) and finding and removing the worm. Cover the wound with moist soil to encourage new roots to form.

5 Another trick is to go out at night and shine a strong light behind the stem and see the outline of the borer. You can take a long needle and stab him to death - very satisfying.

6 If you do suffer damage throw away dead vines in the trash and clean up all residue from the garden to keep them from coming back next year.

Finally, you can consider squash to be a succession plant and instead of planting two plants at a time, plant them a month apart. If your first plant is damaged, pull it up and plant another set of seeds in its place.

Sweet Potatoes

Sweet potatoes are not often grown in a small garden setting because they're inexpensive at the grocery store. But the yellow "*Nancy Halls*" variety I recommend is rarely seen, and is definitely worth the effort. The flesh is pale yellow and the taste is like a buttered white potato with a hint of nutty flavor, with all the health benefits of a normal sweet potato. I learned about yellow sweet potatoes at a South Carolina farmers market. The grower explained that since they damage easily and don't store well, they are seldom grown on commercial farms. A home gardener can handle them more carefully.

Soil
Sweet potatoes like a rich, well-drained soil. No extra fertilizers are needed.

Planting
Sweet potatoes are shipped as "slips" - pencil sized plants with white roots and a few leaves. They may appear to be wilted or unhappy in some way when they arrive, but they're tough and if they are planted right they'll rebound and get off to a good start. Feel free to remove damaged leaves or cut off some of the top stem if needed. In some cases you can cut a slip in half, plant the bottom root and remove the leaves from the bottom of the top plant and plant it as well. These cuttings will root very quickly.

Plant as soon as possible. The best time is later in the day out of the hot sun. If planting must be delayed, remove all the materials (*rubber bands, newspaper, and packing moss*) from the plants and place the roots where they can get some moisture, but avoid wetting the stems and leaves. Folding the roots in damp newspaper works pretty well. If the delay will be more than a few days you can "heel in" sweet potato slips by placing a bunch of them in some potting mix and keeping them watered. They can last this way for a couple of weeks.

When left alone, sweet potatoes will vine along the ground. Wherever a vine's stem hits soil it will try to put down roots, and the roots will develop into potatoes. The vines will crawl all over your garden and you will end up with scores of tiny potatoes. Although they are tasty, they will take over the rest of your garden and interfere with your other crops. In an intensive garden, sweet potatoes are planted closely together and grown up a trellis net. Since they are not natural climbers the gardener will need to arrange the vines manually upward through the netting every week. This is very easy to do and the result is a wonderful set of vines climbing up your trellis.

Wherever a vine's stem hits soil it will try to put down roots, and the roots will develop into potatoes.

Plant each slip so that every one is five inches from its neighbor. This way you can arrange 35 plants in four square feet. Take a trowel and make a deep opening in the soil, place the slip deeply in the soil, removing any leaves that would be below the surface. Firm up the soil and water them all when you're done.

Plant care

Keep an eye on the slips as they take root. Add extra water if they seem wilted in their first few days. If some of your first slips die off, you can cut some of the best plants back and root their cuttings to fill in empty spots in your garden plan. When using this method, it's very important to remember to train the vines up the netting every week.

Harvesting

The sweet potatoes mature at different rates based on the size you desire and growing conditions. The best approach is to wait until the vines are at least 3 feet long and then reach down around the roots of the outermost plants to see how things are going. Sweet potatoes taste good whether they're large or small, so you may want to harvest a few early to get a treat and let others mature to a larger size.

Take care not to damage the potatoes when harvesting. If you break the skin or poke a hole, clean them up and cook them first. Yellow varieties are especially prone to bruising, so take extra care when placing them in baskets. Lightly brush off any extra dirt and stack your "keepers" loosely so they have good ventilation.

Digging for Treasure!

Harvesting sweet potatoes involves all the fun of a treasure hunt combined with the joy of digging in the dirt. Your children will get an up-close look at how the plants and roots grow and how the roots turn into potatoes. The best part is they never know what size potato they'll dig up and what unusual shapes they'll find. Be sure to reward not only the biggest potatoes, but also the tiniest, as well as the most unusual shapes. Take lots of pictures of your kids showing off their treasures.

Storage

The best storage is to keep the potatoes in the ground and only use them as you intend to eat them. Once cold weather approaches or you need your garden space for something else, get your kids to harvest all of the remaining potatoes (*invite the neighborhood kids, too!*). Remember to tell everyone to handle them carefully, brush off loose soil, place them gently in baskets with good ventilation, and cook any damaged potatoes first.

Let the potatoes air dry over the next 8-10 days out of the sun. Then place them in a cool, dark, but well-ventilated area for storage. Don't handle them a lot, just take the top potatoes to eat first.

Cooking

Wash away any remaining dirt from your potatoes and remove anything that doesn't look appealing. Heat your oven to 375° and poke some fork holes in the sides. You might consider placing some aluminum foil on the rack below to catch any drippings. They're done when you squeeze them (*with an oven mitt!*), usually in 35-45 minutes, depending on size. As you gain experience you'll know which settings work best in your kitchen.

Quick Cooking

Sometimes you want sweet potatoes, but don't have a lot of time. Place your potatoes in a covered bowl in the microwave and cook them for about 7 minutes or until they just start to yield when squeezed with a mitt. In the meantime you can preheat your oven to 400°. Finish them in the oven for about another ten minutes, checking occasionally to see if they're done.

Try your yellow sweet potatoes in recipes that call for orange potatoes and see how the taste changes - like sweet potato pie or sweet potatoes and marshmallows.

Tomatoes

Tomatoes are the most popular vegetables grown in the United States. Their fresh taste is so much better than anything you can get in the grocery store that they're almost always in every garden in the country. The problem is that while tomatoes are easy to find and easy to grow, sometimes your results are disappointing. They are susceptible to a host of insects, diseases and wilts. I've seen books that are *entirely* about problems with tomatoes.

The rise in interest in heirloom varieties makes the problem even greater since few are disease resistant. But with a little bit of knowledge and planning, tomatoes can be a winner in your garden every year.

I've been growing tomatoes for over twenty years and have experimented with every possible arrangement of cages, hoops, wires and stakes imaginable. I've learned that there are several elements to consider when growing tomatoes and my results have gotten better each year.

1. Soil

When dealing with any garden, the soil is the first step. Healthy soil means healthy plants, and healthy plants naturally resist diseases and insects. They can sustain damage with little or no loss of productivity, meaning that fertilizers or pesticides are less likely to be needed. Using our system of raised beds, weedless soil and well-balanced, organic fertilizers means you'll eliminate a lot of tomato problems from the start.

2. Raised Beds

They're great for about a dozen reasons – most important is that they allow for better drainage, warmer soil, no compaction of the soil and they are easier to work with.

3. Varieties

Choosing the right varieties is important. I suggest you avoid all the complexities and hassles of trying to start your own plants from seed and stick with transplants. With all the farmers markets and locally run garden centers, it's easy to find the plants you want. There are three main styles - beefsteak/slicing tomatoes for a delicious sandwich, roma/paste tomatoes for stews and sauces, and cherry/grape tomatoes to pop into your salad. What you grow is based on your family's preferences. One plant per person is all you'll usually need and a single cherry tomato can produce enough for a whole family!

I suggest you avoid all the complexities and hassles of trying to start your own plants from seed and stick with transplants.

There are two other considerations - bush/determinant vs. indeterminate and heirloom vs. modern plants. Bush plants grow only so tall and then stop growing. They are best for small gardens with limited space. Indeterminate plants will just keep growing and growing and have a continuous harvest once they mature.

If you're going to grow tomatoes where you've had disease problems before then you should use some of the many newer varieties that have disease resistance built in. Their labels will be clearly marked. Don't worry, they'll still taste great. If you're starting with a new garden or brand new potting mix you can try your hand with the heirlooms - there is a wonderful variety of sizes, shapes, tastes and colors. Experiment with as many as you can fit in your garden and you're guaranteed to have a lot of fun. Next year you can drop the varieties you didn't like and try some others.

Always clean up any dropped leaves, dropped or rotted fruit and put your old plants in the trash, not in your compost pile.

4. Planting times.

Resist the temptation to plant the first day the garden centers get their transplants. Usually that's about a month before the last frost and you're likely to lose your plants to cold weather. Even if they survive they won't thrive. Instead they'll be unhappy and won't produce like the same plants put in at the proper time. Those will take off running and never look back. If you have a spot with good sunlight and you have a raised bed, you can start a week sooner than your neighbors.

5. Plant spacing, air circulation, pruning - stakes vs. cages.

You're well on your way to becoming a tomato master. You have the right soil in a raised bed, you've chosen the right varieties and you're waiting until the perfect time to plant. Next comes the biggest issue, since all tomato plants need support. The question is *"which to use, stakes or cages?"*

I recommend that you use tall stakes and prune your plants to a single main stem.

The key is air circulation. The more you have the fewer problems you'll find with diseases that curl your leaves and kill your plants from the bottom up, just as your fruit is starting to ripen. Wire cages and circles are fine, but the issue is how a tomato naturally grows. It has a main stem and puts out branches, but in the elbows of those branches it also puts out what we call "suckers." These become their own main stems with their own branches and suckers and you quickly end up with a tomato jungle.

I recommend that you use tall stakes and prune your plants to a single main stem. Check every two or three days and pinch off the suckers that appear. It doesn't take that much extra effort and the result is a happier, healthier plant with bigger fruit and fewer problems. I also suggest that as the plant grows, you remove the lower branches to expose the bottom 12" of the main stem. This really improves the air circulation throughout the plant but the main benefit is in resisting wilts and other fungal diseases. The theory is that rainwater hits the ground where the wilt lives and splashes onto the lower leaves of the plant. The leaves get infected and when water hits them, it splashes up to the next level. That's why you should throw away pruned leaves and branches and any dropped or rotted fruit.

In the past I've used eight foot pressure-treated wood stakes that I sink one and a half to two feet into the ground. If you're a purist you could seal them with polyurethane or go with an untreated stake. Recently I've discovered some great stakes that are metal tubes covered with plastic that you can find almost everywhere.

6. Planting transplants.

It's easy. Pinch or clip off the bottom few branches, pop the plants out of their pots and plant a little more deeply than they were originally growing. With a good drink of water they'll be off to a fine start.

Pinch off suckers while they're still small.

Getting Your Tomato Ready to Plant
Tomatoes are one of the few plants that like to be planted below their original soil level.

1. Carefully remove lower branches
2. Plant deeply.
3. As plant grows, remove "suckers" by pinching them off.
4. As plant continues to grow, remove the branches on the bottom 12" of the main stem.

New Planting Depth

7. Tie them up.

As your plants grow up their stakes you'll need to tie them. Look for soft jute twine and cut off 9" lengths in advance. You can loosely tie a bunch to the top of your stakes so you'll have them handy. Wrap around your stake twice and then go under a branch and tie loosely. Resist the urge to tie up your plant too quickly. Let it grow up and strengthen in the breeze first. This will result in a stockier plant with a nice thick stem.

8. Companion plants and interplanting.

Certain plants when put together allow each to grow better, either from encouraging beneficial insects or confusing or repelling the bad bugs. Marigolds and nasturtiums are the best examples for tomatoes. Look for varieties that have a strong smell. Carrots and onions also do well with tomatoes. My experience has taught me that it's better to mix things up in the garden rather than to have everything together. So I plant a tomato, a pepper and an eggplant and then another tomato instead of having all my tomatoes in a row.

9. Mulch, mulch, mulch!

Mulching is great for tomatoes. It keeps the moisture in the soil at an even level, keeps the weeds down, and stops water from splashing up to your plants. Pine needles and pine bark are good choices. A light layer of dried grass clippings is good, but don't let it get too thick. I prefer to use compost as mulch. Weeds don't grow in it and it has the same effects as other mulches, but it also fertilizes the soil.

10. Water

You want to water evenly and thoroughly. Uneven watering causes the fruits to crack and too much water affects the taste. So keep an eye on things and if it hasn't rained and your plants look thirsty, give them a good soaking. It's much better to water deeply every three days than lightly every day.

11. Fertilizing

I don't recommend fertilizer while your plants are growing. What's already in the soil should be fine. But spraying the leaves (*foliar feeding*) is great. You can use various solutions like fish emulsion, or you can make compost tea, which is also great for improving insect and disease resistance.

12. Advanced Tomato Tips!

You all know that I prefer to remove "suckers" from tomato vines and train them as a single stem. Someone asked me if I had ever heard of removing the larger suckers and planting them in order to generate a second crop in late summer. I've discovered an even better way to start a second crop of tomatoes at the end of the summer.

With the single stem system often the plants get too high to handle conveniently. Tomato plants can grow 30 feet tall! The solution is to select a new sucker that is growing from the lower parts of the plant, but instead of clipping it off and planting it by itself, you let it start to grow, still attached to the main stem. Once your *main* plant is too high to reach you can "top it off" by trimming all new growth. This will let the existing fruits grow and continue to ripen while the sucker from below starts to grow. You can then start training it up the main pole.

Once the original plant has finished with all its fruit, you can cut it away completely. This system has the advantage of starting a new plant for late summer and early fall harvest, but the new section has a mature root system from the start. The results are a much larger second harvest in much less time.

Another advanced tomato tip involves a different type of cracking in tomatoes called "sun scald." As the fruits ripen they can expand in the hot sun, causing them to crack and then heal over. A solution is to keep a few properly placed suckers growing and use them as sun umbrellas. They'll shade the fruits and keep them from splitting. Just make sure to trim off any fruiting branches or new branches from your "umbrella sucker."

Finally, harvest the fruits at the most appealing ripeness stage -- up to dead red ripe. Tomato flavor is best at room temperature, but ripe fruit may be held at 45° to 50°F for 7 to 10 days. Follow these tips and your tomatoes will be the envy of the neighborhood!

Welcome to Gardening!

We've come a long way. We've learned how to make a small spot of land in your back yard into a productive garden that takes very little effort. We know about all sorts of different vegetables and how to plant and grow them. And you've involved your children every step of the way. They are going to learn so much! They're trying new foods and will have a new attitude about vegetables and nature that will last a lifetime.

Now you're a gardener and you didn't have to be an expert to be successful. When you see an unusual vegetable on a restaurant menu you can ask about it, or look it up on the Internet. *"Does that grow in my area? Where can I get the seeds? Will it be productive enough to earn a spot for a trial in my garden?"*

Remember that no garden is perfect. Crops will fail from high heat, from too much rain or for no reason at all. But if you try a wide variety of crops every season there will always be something that comes through. If not, you just pull everything out and start again next time and compare notes with your neighbors.

Good luck on your family's journey into healthy living.

QUESTION: Where does a green thumb come from?

ANSWER: Pinching off tomato suckers is a great way to increase your harvest and reduce bacterial and fungal diseases, but it also gives you a green thumb and your hands will smell like tomatoes!

Don.

Index . . . .

About the Author...

Don Rosenberg has memories from his early childhood shelling peas with his grandfather on his back porch and later watching him grow tomatoes in his garden in Florida. Later, as an owner of a chain of retail music stores, he worked from home

and began growing vegetables in his back yard for his own family. He enjoyed the fresh vegetables, but his schedule didn't allow him much time to spend in the garden, so he began a search for ways to make gardening as little work as possible.

After spending 27 years in the music industry, Don Rosenberg was ready for a change. He decided to start a new business based on something he had grown to love – organic gardening. He realized that many people want to grow their own family gardens but don't have a lot of time to spend or the expertise on how to get started.

So, in November of 2006, he founded Instant Organic Garden in Charlotte, North Carolina, and has turned it into a business that makes it easy for anyone to have a garden, even beginners. It's especially appropriate for today's busy lifestyle. Don talks with each family, helps determine the best site for a garden and comes up with a four season garden plan. The beds are installed complete with weedless, organic soil and organic fertilizers. All that remains is planting seeds and watering. He includes twelve months of online, email and phone support. Now he sells his cedar garden kits online across the United States.

This book is a result of his desire to share with others his secrets to successful organic gardening. Don's inspiration comes from clients describing how excited their children are picking and eating delicious vegetables from their new gardens. Parents are asking for more ways they can involve their kids in the whole gardening adventure!

Don Rosenberg received his Bachelor's Degree from the University of Virginia and is a North Carolina Master Gardener. He writes a regular column for a local publication, *The Charlotte Weekly,* called "*Easy Growing.*" He has two teenage sons and enjoys fishing, canoeing, and tennis. He talks to groups on entrepreneurship and business planning as well as gardening.

Don's website is *www.instantorganicgarden.com* and his email is *info@instantorganicgarden.com.*

How Can We Help You?

Instant Organic Garden can help you with every stage of your organic gardening experience...

Garden Planning, Installation and Support.

We install raised bed vegetable gardens in Charlotte, NC and will be adding more affiliates across the country. Go to **www.instantorganicgarden.com** and take our online veggie quiz to indicate your family's level of interest in each possible crop. We'll create a four season garden plan that shows what to grow, when to plant and how much to plant. We'll install your garden complete with weedless soil mix and organic fertilizers along with twelve months support via phone, website and email.

Western Red Cedar Beds

We can ship you your own raised beds or trellis beds made from untreated Western Red Cedar that will last for years and years. The wood is from sustainable forests and weathers to a beautiful silver gray.

Local Affiliates

Contact an Instant Organic Garden affiliate in your area...

North Carolina
Charlotte
Don Rosenberg
704-364-1784
sales@instantorganicgarden.com

For information about becoming an Instant Organic Garden Affiliate or to distribute books or raised bed garden kits, contact Don Rosenberg, 704-364-1784. donrosenberg@gmail.com